ON BASIC HUMAN RIGHTS

OSHO

on basic
human rights

OSHO

This is a new and expanded edition of *On Basic Human Rights* and all
content of this book is selected from various talks by Osho, given to a
live audience. All of Osho's talks have been published in full as books,
and are also available as original audio recordings. Audio recordings
and the complete text archive can be found via the online OSHO
Library at www.osho.com/library

OSHO® and OSHO Vision® are registered trademarks of OSHO
International Foundation www.osho.com/trademarks

OSHO MEDIA INTERNATIONAL
New York – Zurich – Mumbai
an imprint of
OSHO INTERNATIONAL
www.osho.com/oshointernational

Distributed by Publishers Group Worldwide
www.pgw.com

Library of Congress Catalog-In-Publication Data is available

Printed in USA by Bang Printing

ISBN: 978-1-938755-85-9
This title is also available in eBook format ISBN: 978-0-88050-071-5

Contents

Introduction

I happen to live, at the moment, in a part of the world where a significant majority of my neighbors voted for Donald Trump for president of the United States. Many of them for a number of complex, even understandable (on a certain level) reasons. Others simply because they are brainwashed and conditioned in a way that has made them stupid. Among both types of voters—but not all, by any means—are the sorts of people who seek out dictators, who go hand-in-glove with and create them, as Osho describes so eloquently in the early pages of this book.

A few are, knowingly or unknowingly, hoping for the biblical End Times, wherein they hope to be "raptured" into paradise and leave this sinful world behind. Or, in a more secular vein, they are "prepping" for the version of end times where hordes of desperate, starving people will storm their homes to take all of what little they have, killing them in the process if it comes to that.

On the bigger-picture level, angry young white men in America march in the streets bearing torches and flinging Nazi salutes, dressed in the costumes and rhetoric of Hitler and his army of followers in 1930s Germany. A ceaseless and smoldering "war on terror," initiated by America and its allies, terrorizes millions of human beings in the Middle East and beyond, who flee in fear and grief from the only homes they have ever known. Eruptions of nationalism, resurgences of tribalism, people feeling threatened and afraid, drawing their boundaries ever more tightly and imperviously around themselves.

Day by passing day, one cannot help but feel that we are coming face-to-face with a momentous crossroads in our evolution as a human species on this planet we share. This book could not have come at a better time.

Unlike many so-called "spiritual teachers," Osho has never shied away from dealing with politics and its politicians, academia and its pretensions, the "masses" and their beliefs and superstitions. (And if you think he is a "teacher," he will set you straight in the chapter called Freedom and Love, The Center and Circumference.) He is not, and has never been, an airy-fairy, "just-think-positive-and-it-will-be-alright" kind of guy. Not by a long shot.

He is just the kind of guy, in other words, whose clear-eyed, no-nonsense insights into the nature of human beings, and for that matter, into reality itself—as it is, not as we have been told we should think it is—is very much needed at this time.

The book begins with an incisive critique of the much-heralded, often-quoted "Universal Declaration of Human Rights" passed by members of the United Nations. Signed on December 10, 1948, the declaration was at best an effort to make a statement about what it means to be human, to be civilized, to be free, following the horrors of the Second World War. Osho takes a fresh and uncon-ventional, even contrarian, look at this well-intentioned document from the previous century. He then offers his own, twenty-first century proposal for universal human rights, and from there we hear what he has to say about the Charter for the United Nations itself, both in its aspirations and its failures. (Both documents are provided for your reference in the Appendix.)

The remainder of the book, titled "Starting Over: Roadmaps for a Revolution in Consciousness," is a compilation of pieces that add more dimension to the insights offered at the beginning. These chap-ters are chosen from his many talks in response to questions, selected to serve as a kind of survival manual for the "resistance," or to provide maps to help locate ourselves along the roads and byways leading to this crossroads we face now, both collectively and individually.

If we are, in fact, presented with an urgent challenge to transform ourselves and the ways we relate to one another on this Earth we all share, where are we now? In what ways do we need to wake up, grow up, become more fully human? And what tools do we need to start the work of taking responsibility for creating a human life and civilization that is worthy of the name.

Sarito Carol Neiman, editor and compiler

The Universal Declaration of Human Rights: What Does it Mean?

Osho,
Would it not be better if you were to talk only about spirituality?
Why do you bring politics and other subjects into it?

> *I look at life in its totality and that total vision is what I call*
> *spirituality. Politics is one of the subjects, and so is*
> *mathematics, and human rights.*
> *Spirituality is not a single category; spirituality means life in*
> *its totality. Spirituality means knowing and living life in its*
> *totality. Politics can live in its own category and so can*
> *mathematics, but not spirituality because spirituality does*
> *not have a category of its own. It is the art of living this life*
> *as a whole. It touches every part of life. Of course, politics*
> *would not like spirituality to touch it; nor would science or*
> *commerce—because spirituality changes whatever it*
> *touches. The moment the reflection of spirituality falls on*
> *politics, it cannot remain the same; similarly, science and*
> *commerce cannot remain what they are. It is to their*
> *advantage that spirituality does not touch them, but it is not*
> *good for spirituality.*
> *The moment spirituality is divided into segments, it becomes*
> *lifeless and pale. It can remain healthy only in its*
> *wholeness.*
> *That does not mean spirituality has to become political, or*
> *anything else. It does not have to become anything; its*
> *reflection is enough. It has only to look at politics,*
> *commerce, and science. Its vision and its wakefulness itself*
> *are a revolution.*
> *I am trying to follow this course, and will continue to do so.*
> *But many vested interests are afraid of that. They even want*
> *to define the limits of spirituality.*

*That is only to save themselves and to destroy spirituality.
An institution that depends on exploiting people would not
like spirituality to take an interest in the totality of life
because spirituality cannot tolerate exploitation—and any
spirituality that does tolerate it is impotent. Actually the
spirituality that is prevalent is not spirituality at all, but a
kind of pseudo-spirituality. That kind of spirituality has
acted only as a hallucinogen and I don't want to be
included in anything like that.
As far as the promotion of spirituality is concerned, I am not
interested in any sort of propaganda. In fact, man has to be
freed from all kinds of propaganda.
Consciousness can understand only that which rises above
all such propaganda. Propaganda is conditioning, whereas
spirituality is deconditioning.
You can have political propaganda, but not spiritual
propaganda. Those who publicize spirituality are nothing
but politicians in disguise.
I am neither a promoter nor a preacher. I want to shatter
everyone's sleep. I want to shake people out of their
unconsciousness, so they can see and think for themselves.
I don't want to think for them. A preacher does that. A
promoter does that. They make everyone fall asleep because
only those who are asleep will trust them and make them
leaders and masters. A person who is awake will find his
own way. He does not become anyone's student or follower.
Only unconscious people can be students and followers. Of
course, people become angry if they are woken up but I am
happy with that—because it is the beginning of their
awakening.*

Celebrating the UN Declaration:
An Exercise in Hypocrisy

Osho,
It feels strange when the establishment worldwide, which is ever busy with all its efforts and resources to resist any change that would threaten its power, asks us to celebrate "Human Rights Day." What is going on?

One of the most fundamental things to be always remembered is that we are living in a hypocrite society.

Once, a great philosopher was asked, "What do you think of civilization?" The philosopher said, "It is a good idea, but somebody has to change the idea into a reality. Civilization has not happened yet. It is a dream of the future." But the people who are in power—politically, religiously, socially—are in power because civilization has not happened. A civilized world, a mature human being needs no nations—all those boundaries are false—needs no religions, because all those theologies are simple fictions.

The people who have been for thousands of years in power—the priests, the politicians, the super-rich—have all the powers to prevent human evolution. The best way to prevent it is to convince people, "You are already civilized," to convince them, "You are already a human being. You need not go through a transformation, it is unnecessary." And man's weakness is that knowing perfectly well there exists no such thing as civilization, there exists no such thing as human sensitivity, still he starts believing in all the lies that the politicians have been speaking, the priests have been preaching, the educationists have been teaching—because it seems simpler to just believe. You don't have to do anything for it.

To recognize the fact that you are not yet human creates fear. The very ground underneath your feet disappears. Truth makes you utterly naked—naked of all lies, naked of all hypocrisies. That's why nobody wants truth. Everybody believes that he has got it.

Do you see the psychological strategy? If you don't want to give something to someone, convince him, hypnotize him, repeat again and again, "You have got it." And when thousands of people around you—your parents, your teachers, your priests, your leaders—are all believing it, it seems almost impossible for new arrivals in the world, small children, not to be convinced of this thousands-of-years-old idea. Millions of people have lived and died believing that civilization has happened.

So the first thing I want you to understand is that we are still barbarous. Only barbarians can do things that we have been doing for thousands of years—not human beings. In three thousand years, five thousand wars . . . and you call man civilized? In the twentieth century—exactly in the middle of the twentieth century—you can produce Adolf Hitler, you can produce Joseph Stalin, you can produce Benito Mussolini, you can produce Mao Zedong. And still you believe man is civilized?

Adolf Hitler alone killed six million human beings, and killed with great sophistication. Science and technology have been used; one million Jews have been simply killed in gas chambers; within seconds, thousands of people are nothing but smoke going out of the chimneys. He killed so many people that it was impossible to give each person a conventional grave. Man has never been so poor— even beggars have graves, but Hitler had killed so many people that to make graves for all of them . . . the whole of Germany would have become a graveyard. So he had deep ditches prepared, and people were simply thrown into the ditches and covered with mud. Before throwing their bodies in the ditches he destroyed even those dead peoples' dignity. Their clothes were taken away; their heads, their beards, their moustaches were shaved so you could not recognize the face of the person. Their heads were cut off, so you would find somewhere the head and somewhere the hand and somewhere the leg and somewhere the remaining parts of the body. And thousands of people . . . it was impossible to identify who you were looking for.

Why did he do that? So that nobody could be recognized. Even if somebody was found dead, he could not be recognized; he did not even have his whole body. And you say that man is civilized?

And this is not the end of the story. Seeing the Second World War, one would have thought that just a little intelligence is needed and the Second World War should be the last world war—seeing what man himself has been doing to man. But no, we are preparing for the third world war—and the last.

Albert Einstein was asked, "Can you say something about what is going to happen in the third world war?" And Einstein said, "Excuse me, I cannot say anything about the third world war, but I can say something about the fourth." The questioner could not believe it. He said, "You cannot say anything about the third—and it is so complicated—yet you are ready to say something about the fourth, which will be even more complicated?"

Albert Einstein said, "You don't understand. I can say something definitively, categorically, about the fourth. And that is that the fourth is never going to happen, because the third will destroy all life—not only human beings, roses too. All that is living will disappear from the earth."

And you say that humanity has become civilized? No, you have been deceived, and this Universal Declaration of Human Rights by the United Nations is nothing but the same hypocrisy.

George Gurdjieff used to tell a small story—but it is about humanity. The story is that there was a magician. He lived deep in the mountains and the forests, and he had thousands of sheep. But the problem was that the sheep were afraid of the magician, because every day the sheep were seeing that one of them was being killed for his breakfast, another was being killed for his lunch. So they used to run away from the magician's place, and it was a difficult job to find them in the vast forest. Being a magician, he used magic. He hypnotized all the sheep and told different sheep . . . to some, "You are a man, you need not be afraid. It is only the sheep who are going to be killed and eaten, not you. You are a man just like I am." Some other sheep were told, "You are a lion—only sheep are afraid. They escape, they are cowards. You are a lion; you would prefer to die than to run away. You don't belong to these sheep. So when they are killed it is not your problem. They are meant to be killed, but you are the most loved of my friends in this forest."

In this way he told every sheep different stories, and from the second day, the sheep stopped running away from the house. They still saw other sheep being killed, butchered, but it was not their concern. Somebody had been told he was a lion, somebody was a tiger, somebody was a man . . . Nobody was a sheep except the one who was being killed. This way, without keeping servants, the magician managed thousands of sheep. They would go into the forest for their food, for their water, and they would come back home, believing always one thing: "It is some sheep who is going to be killed, not you. You don't belong to this mob. You are a lion—respected, honored, a friend of the great magician." Thus, the problems of the magician were solved.

I am telling you this story because it is literally true about you. You are being told things and you accept them, without even looking all around to see whether those things coincide with the reality or not.

The first thing . . .

My first objection to the UN's Declaration of Human Rights is that rights exist only when there are duties. Duties are roots, rights are the flowers; you cannot have rights without duties. And to celebrate a day in the year for human rights . . . but they don't celebrate a day for human duties, which comes first.

Why are they not talking about human duties? Because they don't want to give you your human rights! Without duties, rights can only be talked about, but you won't have them in your hands. And about duties, these politicians who have made this declaration have no notion at all. I will give you a few examples.

They say that every human being is equal. And of course it satisfies the ego of every human being—nobody objects. It is one of the most dangerous lies to tell human beings. I say to you, equality is a myth. There are not even two human beings who are equal in any way, in any dimension.

I don't mean that they are unequal—I mean that they are unique, incomparable, so the question of equality or inequality does not arise. Are you equal to these pillars in the hall? The pillars may be beautiful, but you are not equal to them. But does that mean you are inferior to the pillars? It simply means you are not a pillar—pillars are pillars, you are you.

Every human being is a category unto himself. And unless we recognize the uniqueness of each individual, there are not going to be any human rights, and there is not going to be a civilized world—human, loving, rejoicing.

In the declaration they emphasize the fact again and again that you should love all human beings; you are all brothers. But have you ever seen brothers being in love? Have you ever seen brothers being friends? The way brothers fight, nobody fights! And just saying, "You are brothers," does not make it a reality.

These people who declared these human rights—what authority have they got? Who are they? Politicians! And they are the cause of all the wars, they are the cause of all kinds of violence happening all over the world. These are the people who have kept almost half of humanity, womankind, in a state of slavery. But looking at the declaration, I had really a great time . . . because it does not talk about sisters, only brothers. Sisters don't count, yet they are half of humanity. They are not even mentioned.

These politicians are articulate, clever, cunning, mostly coming from the legal profession. They are saying there should be no discrimination between man and woman, between black and white; between races, religions, political ideologies, there should be no discrimination. And who is making the discrimination? These are the same people who are making the declaration! They have enslaved the woman for centuries, and they are not yet willing to give her freedom—which, according to their declaration, is a basic human right. And blacks are being treated as animals.

Just at the end of the 19th century, black people were still being sold, auctioned in marketplaces like a commodity. And even today they are not respected as the white people are respected. But these are the white people—all these politicians are white. These white people have been driving the whole of humanity, for three hundred years, into slavery.

They all had their empires. England had the biggest empire; it was said that the sun never set in the British Empire. Somewhere or other in the British Empire the sun was shining and it was day, all around the earth. And other white people were not far behind: the French, the Portuguese, the Spanish—they all had vast empires, exploiting the whole earth. They have been the parasites—and it is hilarious that all these parasites are now declaring human rights.

This is a deception. It is not meant; what they are saying, they don't mean. It is just to give you an idea that you are equal to everybody, you are a brother to everybody, that you have all the human rights. But I know—all these human rights are just hypocrisies. I know by my own experience.

There is one human right enumerated in this declaration: nobody can be arrested without a warrant. I was arrested exactly like that in America—without a warrant, without any arrest warrant or search warrant. Not even verbally did they inform me what crime I had committed. And when I asked them, "What crime have I committed? I must know at least," the answer was loaded guns—twelve loaded guns surrounding my jet airplane. When guns are answers, then you can be certain that civilization is far away.

They did not have any arrest warrant. But they not only arrested me, they were clever: they had deliberately arrested me at such a time that I would have to be in jail for at least two days. On Monday the court would open, only then could I be bailed out. They themselves were certain that I would be bailed out, because there was no reason to hold me; they didn't have any proof, any evidence against me. They had chosen a certain situation in which for two days the court was closed—so at least they would have the satisfaction of torturing me for two days. On the third day, I was not surprised when the court refused to give me bail. The magistrate, a woman, did not even allow my attorneys to question the fact that I had been arrested without any arrest warrant. In a democratic country, which claims to be the greatest democratic country in the world, the court would not allow them even to discuss it, because to discuss it would be an exposure. There was no question of giving me bail. In the first place I had been arrested without any warrant—and even after three days they didn't have the warrant—the question of bail should not even arise, but the bail was not given.

In the second court, a higher federal court, again the question, what about my arrest?—which is the basic question—was not discussed. Everything else is secondary. First, you arrest somebody without even telling him why he is being arrested. . . . And in these human rights, these same politicians sitting in America say that nobody can be arrested without an arrest warrant; this is a "fundamental human right." If I had not been arrested, I might not have known.

They say nobody should interfere in anybody's philosophy, religion, political ideology—that is every individual's birthright. But my commune in America was destroyed for the simple reason that

Christianity . . . My being not a white man, my commune being universal . . . there were black people, there were people from all over the world. It was the only place where there was no discrimination of any kind. They destroyed a commune which was fulfilling human rights in every detail.

On the surface man has become civilized, but deep in the darker parts of his unconsciousness he is still barbarous.

In the introduction to this declaration it says, "We are determined to eliminate all forms of intolerance and of discrimination based on religion or belief." And this is not true in any country. Religions are fighting continuously, and if the government consists of fanatic religious people, the minority is crushed and destroyed in every possible way.

The desire is good, but the people who are desiring it are all wrong.

In the convention at which the United Nations declared these fundamental rights, the Soviet Union was absent; eight other communist countries were absent. America was present. Unanimously the declaration was adopted—all in favor and nobody against. I am mentioning it because it was basically an American initiative to make this declaration. And America is the first to be going against every human right.

America gave two hundred million dollars to the terrorists in Nicaragua, a small country which had become communist, just like Cuba. To destroy the country, America flooded it with terrorists. Millions of dollars were being poured in continuously, to support the terrorists with weapons and everything. And in this declaration it says that every country is sovereign, and no other country should interfere in any other country's life and religion. That is their business, how they want to live, what they want to believe or not to believe. It is nobody else's business at all. If in some small country people have accepted communism as their lifestyle and their social structure, who is America?—and what right have they?

Nicaragua appealed to the World Court; and the World Court is full of American judges. Still the World Court said to America, "Your act is against the Human Rights Declaration, it is criminal." Ronald Reagan simply cancelled it. He said, "We don't care about the World Court or their decisions."

Now, these are the people who have made the declaration—they have created the World Court to decide in situations where some conflict arises, and these same people are not ready to listen.

Do you see the politics behind it? The World Court, the declaration—all are facades to hide things. If some small country were doing what America did, then the World Court would be right, and America would have taken action in favor of the World Court to destroy that country because it was doing a criminal act. Now, because America itself is doing the criminal act, it simply can say, "We don't care about the World Court."

And what can the World Court do? It has no armies, it has no power. It has all the power that has been given by the politicians, but if those politicians themselves go against the law that they have made, what can the court do? And the UN is silent! Its court has been insulted; if the people in the UN have any dignity they will dissolve the UN and dissolve the World Court—because what is the point? Today America is doing it, tomorrow other countries will. And the Soviet Union was far better and was right, because it never participated in this declaration. It was not part of this declaration; no communist government participated in it. So at least they have shown from the very beginning that these things are all bogus: "Whom are you trying to cheat?"

All the rights are, in a way, not very rational. For example, in this long declaration there is no mention of the right to leave the body when one has lived enough and is now weak, sick, old, a burden, and of no use. One is suffering unnecessarily and waiting for death. Why wait? Why put this person unnecessarily in torture? The society is responsible for thousands of people who are in torture, in hospitals or in nursing homes. They don't have any possibility of coming back to life healthy, creative, of any use, but they can go on vegetating. Medicine is developed enough that you can keep them in the hospitals for years. Artificial breathing . . . perhaps the man is already dead, but because of the artificial breathing you are deceived.

In this long list, one of the most important human rights is not included, and that right is the right to leave the world. To give the ticket back, to say, "I want to go back home: who are you to prevent me, or anybody?" But that right . . . which is very significant today, because in the advanced countries, the average life span has gone to such lengths. More and more people will be in a situation where their sons and daughters are already old, eighty, ninety; the fourth or fifth or sixth generation has already arrived. And that fifth or sixth generation cannot have any connection with a person 120 years old, just vegetating in a hospital. Those new arrivals have no relationship, they don't have any respect. Now, months pass and those old people are hanging around in the hospitals waiting, hoping that somebody may come—a friend, a child, an old acquaintance—to meet them. Nobody comes. People avoid them. They are boring, naturally. It is almost as if you are reading a fifty-year-old newspaper. They don't have anything new; everything is fifty, sixty years old. If you go to them they will talk only about those golden days when they used to be young and life was an adventure. You cannot connect with them, and you feel simply bored. Everything has changed in fifty years, and those people are not even aware of what has changed. But euthanasia, the right to die—in this long declaration, it is not included.

Politicians are very, very cunning. They don't want to be controversial, so they say only things which you like, or everybody is going to like. They are not concerned with the actual situation and the changes it needs. Their whole effort is in how to make you happy just by giving you bogus words.

Nowhere in the world are any of the basic rights being applied.

I will go through a few important rights:

Whereas disregard and contempt for human rights has resulted in barbarous acts which have outraged the conscience of mankind...

It has two implications in it. One is that the people who made this declaration have accepted that humanity is civilized; that's why once in a while, if there is any barbarous act, those human beings in the world, the whole of mankind, suffers in conscience, feels the pain, the anguish.

Both are lies, because I don't see humanity having any conscience. When Muslims kill Hindus, no Muslim thinks that he has done wrong—the question of conscience does not arise. In fact, according to his religion he has done some virtuous act. He was trying to convert the Hindus to Islam, because if you are not a Muslim you cannot enter paradise. He was trying to help you in every possible way, to smuggle you, rightly or wrongly, into paradise; from the front door or from the back door, it doesn't matter. But you are resistant, you don't want to go to paradise, you are deter- mined to go to hell—that's why he prevents you, he beheads you. It is better to be killed by the hands of a religious Muslim. The Koran says the man who is killed by Muslims will enter paradise, just as the Muslims who have killed him will enter paradise. So they are really trying to save people from going to hell—why should they feel any pain in their conscience?

No Hindu feels it, no Christian feels it. Christians have killed more people than anybody else, and particularly they have burned living people. Others have been killing and then burning; Christianity has a shortcut, why make it in two parts? When the book can be published in one book, why make two volumes? First kill the man and then burn him?—burn him directly! Thousands of people have been burned alive. I don't see anywhere that anybody is outraged.

If people were outraged things would change—because who is doing them? We are doing them. This sentence in the beginning of the declaration is such a lie. First it says "barbarous acts"—in fact, in these past decades we have done more barbarous acts than in the whole history of man. In ten thousand years we have not been able to do so many barbarous activities as we have done just within fifty, sixty years. We are becoming more and more barbarous—of course with a style and method.

Hiroshima and Nagasaki—what do you think? Are these bar- barous acts, or are they an effort to send the beautiful people of Nagasaki and Hiroshima directly to paradise together? Whole cities, more than two hundred thousand people, entered within five min- utes—I don't think there was ever such a crowd at the gates of para- dise! And it was America that was responsible for Hiroshima and Nagasaki. It is now absolutely confirmed by the people who under- stand military science that dropping the atom bombs on Hiroshima and Nagasaki was absolutely useless. Japan was already surren- dering—Germany had surrendered, and now there was no possibility that Japan could go on fighting; not for more than one week, or maybe not even that long. Seeing that Germany was finished, Japan could not fight alone. It is a small country of very courageous people, brave people, but a very small country. It was fighting with the support of Germany, and when the main support disappeared, Japan was going to surrender.

And this was the fear of President Truman of America: Japan

may surrender tomorrow; then he will miss the chance to drop the atom bombs. And they had put so much money and energy and genius into creating atom bombs, they wanted to try them. Man is not important, but money—their bombs had to be tried. And you say that because of barbarous acts, the civilized people feel a prick of conscience? Was President Truman a civilized man or not? Even his own military experts had told him that it was absolutely meaningless, unnecessarily destroying human life. But he went ahead.

The next morning hundreds of journalists had gathered at the White House to see President Truman, because the world's greatest catastrophe created by man had happened. Their first question was, "Mr. President, did you have a good sleep?"—because he had gone to bed only after he had received the message: "Hiroshima and Nagasaki are in smoke, they are no longer on the map of the earth." Then he went to bed; otherwise he would have waited for the news to reach him. He said, "Yes, I slept more peacefully than ever, because our experiment has succeeded. Now we are the greatest power in the world."

And you are talking about conscience? More than two hundred thousand people died within three minutes, and the man whose order killed them slept very "peacefully," as he had never slept before. And if this is the situation of President "True-Man," then what about the people who are not such true men?

As far as I am concerned, civilization is still a dream, a hope, a utopia. If we don't fall for the tricks of the magician and start believing that we are civilized people, this hope can become a reality, the dream can become a concrete experience.

And conscience arises only after meditation, never before it. You are not born with a conscience. You can watch small children: If they see an ant, they will kill it. Do you think the small child has some conscience? Do you think the small child is a criminal, a murderer? No, nothing like that. It is just out of curiosity, he's just exploring his world. He has entered a new world, and he is exploring it. But there is no question of conscience. He does not feel that when he has been beating a dog for no reason, the dog also feels pain. Children don't have any conscience; they have only seeds.

All these politicians are trying to convince humanity: "You have a conscience." You don't have. You will have to grow it, you will have to work upon yourself. You will have to learn how to be silent and how to listen to the still, small voice within. I don't think any of the politicians who made this declaration have had any experience of what conscience is, of what consciousness is. It comes only after a long, long pilgrimage inward. You are not given everything by birth. You are given by birth only the necessary things for survival. Everything else is given only as a seed.

If you are intentionally interested in evolving your consciousness to its highest peak, then it is up to you. Nature provides only for survival—not life, not joy, not silence, not ecstasy, not love. Nature can manage itself with only lust—what is the need for love? Why create complications? Love you will have to find, consciousness you will have to grow. You will have to become a gardener of your own being—your being is your garden.

Your being is the Garden of Eden talked about in the Bible. That Garden of Eden is not somewhere else on some other star; it is within you. You have been thrown out of it, and you have been running all around but never going in. The moment you go in, you are back in the Garden of Eden. But now, nobody has taken care of it for thousands of years. You have never been back inside. Everything has gone to seed; now nothing blossoms, no foliage, no greenery. But you can bring it back to life because everything is potentially there.

These people don't understand what conscience is. They have learned only words.

I have heard:

A psychologist was appearing for an oral examination for his doctorate. There were three examiners. The first question they asked was: "What are the most important qualities of the human mother's milk?"

The psychologist was a little puzzled: "What has psychology to do with mother's milk? I have not come here to be an expert in milk products or anything. But what to do, I have to answer." So he said, "First, it has all the nutrients for the child's growth—it is perfect food. Second, it comes from within the mother's body, so it is warm, easily digestible; and because it comes from within, it cannot be carrying any infection, any disease which may be around. The child is protected."

They said, "Right! Now, the third?"

There was a moment of silence because he could not figure it out—what is the third? The first two also he had made up. The third was coming up again and again in his mind, but he was repressing it. When he could not find anything else, he had to say it. He said, "The third is that it comes in nice containers!"

Now, these idiots are going to be psychologists! That was the first thing that had come to his mind—"nice containers."

Looking at the declaration, my first feeling was that these people are articulate, they can play with words. They can use beautiful words which influence you and deceive you—and hide the reality.

Article One: All human beings are born free.

This is absolutely nonsense. If all human beings are born free, leave a child in freedom: he will die within twenty-four hours! Man's child is the most helpless child in the whole world. What freedom can he have? He cannot walk, he cannot talk, he cannot fly. In fact, one scientist had the idea—and I feel some sympathy with his idea— that the human child is born earlier than he should be. He needs at least nine months more in the mother's womb because he is not complete, he's still growing. You see animals' kids—most of them are born and immediately start walking around and searching for food. They are more independent, they are more complete. For the human child it is impossible to survive without the support of the mother and the father and the family or other human beings. What freedom can he have? This is what I say is the most cunning part of the politician's mind: He is giving you the idea that you don't need freedom. "Don't ask for freedom. You are born free; all human beings are born free."

All human beings are born utterly helpless and dependent. It may take years for them to be free. Then too, millions of people never become free. This declaration is saying that they are born free—I am saying millions of people die, and even then they are not free! And you know it from your life: you are not free. The husband is there, the wife is not free. The wife is there, the husband is not free. I have seen husbands and wives walking on the road—the husband is not even free to look here and there! He looks straight ahead, like a Buddhist monk, just four feet ahead. And his wife is looking out of the corner of her eye to see where he is. What kind of freedom is this? The moment the husband reaches home, the first question is: "Where have you been?"—and you are a free man—"Why are you late?"

When I was in school, I was usually late. Life outside was so beautiful, and around my school there were so many mango trees. And when the mango season comes, just to pass by the side of mango trees . . . such fragrance, such sweetness in the air; the mango is certainly the king of all the fruits. There were other fruit trees too, and I was mostly in those trees rather than in class. On the first day when I reached middle school, I was half an hour late. The teacher said, "This won't do. At least with me, this will not do. If you have to study my subject, you have to be here before I come into the class—five minutes earlier. Why are you late?"

I said, "Listen—just because of this question I am not going to get married!"

He said, "What? How does the question of marriage arise?"

I said, "I will explain to you: I have been hearing it everywhere in my neighborhood. Every wife is asking, 'Where have you been? Why are you late?' and I have decided that these questions I am not going to answer. So I am sacrificing my whole life—I'm not going to get married—because of this question, and you think I will answer it for you? I would rather change the subject. Good-bye!"

He said to the class, "This is a strange boy. He brings in irrelevant things—marriage? What has marriage to do with my subject, geography?" But he became interested in me. After school he caught hold of me and he said, "Now, we can sit. I want to understand what is the matter, why?"

I said, "Nobody has the right to ask me why I am late, where I have been. It is my life—if I want to spoil it, it is my right. You are only a servant to teach geography. You are not there to ask such questions to create dependence in me. I hate such questions. I can leave the school; I can completely forget about being educated, there is no need. Because if Jesus, without being educated, can experience himself; if Kabir, without being educated, can know the ultimate . . . I am not interested in any business, in any service, in any employment, so if you want me in your class you will have to be a little more human, not continuously interfering in my freedom."

This first article says, "All human beings are born free." These are the strategies of hypnotizing and conditioning humanity. They have given you the idea that you are born free. Now there is no need to fight for freedom, there is no need to create an inner revolution which makes you really free—free from everything, free from the body, because the body is a bondage. The East is far more truthful. It says you are born in bondage, not that you are born free. Your body is a prison, and your mind and your brain are prisons. Your consciousness is confined in a very small space, and your consciousness is capable of spreading all over the universe. Because you don't know the potential, you think this is all you are.

These people, according to me, are criminals, greater criminals than those who go to the gallows, because they are deceiving the whole of humanity. But the deception is very clever: "You are born free." Naturally, freedom is not a question—not something to be created, to be deserved, to be earned, to be worthy of—you are already free!

George Gurdjieff is the only man in the whole of history who has said such a tremendously significant thing: "You don't have any soul." Now, throughout the whole world, all the religions believe that you have a soul, that you come with a soul. George Gurdjieff's voice is alone in the whole of history, saying that not all men have a soul; the place of the soul is empty. There is a possibility—you can work, you can create the soul, but you are not born with it.

I know, and Gurdjieff knows, that you are born with a soul—but the idea that we are born with a soul has not been helpful. It has made people more asleep: "We are born with a soul, God is within you, the kingdom of God is within you, so what do you have to do?" Things that are not within you, work hard to get them—money, power, respectability—because nobody says, "Every child is born with money, every child is born with political power, every child is born with respectability." Nobody will say that. These things have to be earned.

Freedom, consciousness, God—whatever you call it—has to be discovered. It is hidden, dormant; it has to be made dynamic, has to be made fully mature. It should be brought to flower and fruition. But to tell people, "You are born free—and equal in dignity and rights" . . . People can go on lying so smoothly, with such beautiful words—destroying those words.

Nobody is equal. This is a psychological truth.

Neither in your body nor in your mind nor in your talents, nor among your geniuses—nobody is equal. A Sigmund Freud is a Sigmund Freud, a Bertrand Russell is a Bertrand Russell, a D. H. Lawrence is a D. H. Lawrence. There is not even one other D. H.

Lawrence, and never will be. Each individual is unique.

This idea of equality is so ugly, but it has become almost the religion of the contemporary humanity. "Equality"—I say to you, it is the most destructive idea that has penetrated the human mind. You have to be reminded about your uniqueness.

All human beings are endowed with reason and conscience and should act toward one another in a spirit of brotherhood.

These are all assumptions without any validity. All human beings are not born with reason, are not endowed with reason. For example, there are people, very few . . . I have just named Bertrand Russell; he can be said to be endowed with reason. J. Krishnamurti is another. But ordinary people are living with all kinds of superstitions. Unless you have dropped all your superstitions, you cannot be said to be a rational person.

All Christians believe—and among the whole group of politicians who have drawn up this declaration, ninety percent of them are Christians—they all believe that Jesus is born of a virgin mother. And these are rational beings? He is crucified, and he's resurrected too. He makes dead people come back to life—and these are the fundamentals on which the faith of a Christian depends. Just take a few things out—it is very strange—and you will find Christianity to be the most irreligious religion, the poorest as far as religiousness is concerned. The virgin birth—cancel it, if you have reason. Resurrection—cancel it, if you have reason. Walking on water—cancel it. Raising the dead back to life—cancel it. Changing water into alcohol—not only cancel it but find the guy and give him to the police, because it is a crime, it is not a miracle! But if all these things are canceled, what remains of Christianity? That is the poverty of Christianity.

In Buddhism, you cannot cancel anything because nothing is based on superstition. Buddha himself has canceled anything that smells of superstition—it is just pure rationality.

But to say that man is "endowed with reason" by birth . . . it doesn't seem so. Looking at the world, it doesn't seem that it is a rational world. We have not been living according to reason, we have been living according to all kinds of irrational things. But these are sweet words to believe, that you are "endowed with reason." The more idiotic you are, the more you will believe it, and sooner. . . .

" . . . and conscience, and should act toward one another in a spirit of brotherhood." Conscience arises only after deep meditation, never before it. It is a flowering of meditation. Only very few people in the whole world, in the whole of history, have been conscious, have had conscience. Both the words mean the same, but because of religious people, in all the languages except French they have created different meanings for the two words. Only in French are conscience and consciousness one word. It means the same thing. Religions around the world have tried to take "conscience" separately from consciousness for a certain reason: consciousness comes only after meditation. How long can you deceive people? It is just like when you bring light into the room, and darkness disappears. The moment you are in a meditative state, you have consciousness, awareness. The religions created another word, "conscience." And conscience is what the priests, the church, the religion, teach you about what is good, what is bad, what is virtuous, what is sin—all these teachings make your "conscience." It is a very clever trick to separate conscience from consciousness.

There can be no conscience without consciousness. But they have created a false, artificial "conscience."

For example, I was born in a very ancient religion—perhaps the most ancient, it is a small religion as far as numbers are concerned. But they have their superstitions. Up to the age of eighteen I had not seen a tomato in my house. Do you think tomatoes are dangerous people? But because the color of the tomato is the color of meat, that was enough to debar it. Up to the age of eighteen I had never eaten in the night, because it is prohibited by that religion. You can eat only between sunrise and sunset. Eating in the night you may eat some insect, some ant: some violence may happen. So it is better to eat in light, in full light.

When I was eighteen my friends were going to see a beautiful castle close by, a few miles away. I went with them. I had no idea, I had not even thought about it, but going up the hill to the castle . . . and it was so beautiful, so old, and there were so many things to see, that nobody was ready to prepare food. I asked, "Do something—soon the sun will be setting and I am feeling very hungry, you are feeling hungry. The whole day long we have been moving on the mountain! It has been tiring, but it has been an experience."

They said, "As long as the sun is there, we don't want to miss. There are a few more things to see."

I was the only one who was not accustomed to eating in the night. They were all eating at night, so there was no question. By nine or ten o'clock in the night, they had prepared such delicious food—and particularly after the whole day's hunger, starvation, and moving on the mountain, I was in a dilemma—what to do? Then I told them: "There is a great difficulty. I have never eaten in the night, and the religion in which unfortunately I have been born thinks that if you eat in the night you will go to hell. I don't want to go to hell just for one night's food, but I if I am hungry I cannot sleep either. Moreover, the smell of your food is too much!"

They persuaded me, saying, "We will not tell your parents or anybody. Nobody will ever know that you have eaten in the night."

I said, "That is not the point—I will know. The question is not my parents or anybody. You can tell the whole world, that's not the problem. The problem is that I cannot conceive of myself eating at night after eighteen years of continuous conditioning." But they persuaded me—and I had to be persuaded. I ate, but I could not sleep; I had to vomit the whole night. Now, nobody else vomited. Twenty persons were with me; they all slept—they were tired, they had eaten good food. They slept well. I had to remain awake the whole night, vomiting. Until I was completely clean of the food, I could not sleep. It was just in the morning near about five that I went to sleep.

That gave me the idea that perhaps eating in the night is dangerous. Just one time, and the whole night became hell! And those who have been eating in the night for their whole lives . . . Perhaps the idea that they go to hell is right, but the whole world is eating in the night—if it is true, then everybody will be going to hell! And these twenty friends were sleeping so beautifully, nobody had vomited, so nothing was wrong with the food. And nothing was wrong with those people! Something is wrong in my conditioning, I had been brought up with a wrong idea. But once you accept something, this creates a false conscience that goes on telling you, "Don't do this, do this."

This is not consciousness. Consciousness simply knows what to do, what not to do. There is no question of choice. Consciousness is a choiceless state—you simply know what is right.

You are not born with conscience. It has been created by the religions, and they have exploited you through creating conscience. It is time that we should drop the word *conscience* because it has become associated with a long past and has wrong connotations. You should use the word *consciousness.*

But consciousness is the fragrance of your becoming absolutely silent. It does not come with your birth. Yes, if you can attain consciousness, you will have a new birth; you will be reborn.

That's what Jesus meant when he said to Nicodemus, "Unless you are born again, you will not understand me." He does not mean in your next life. He means that you will have to transform your being, rise in your consciousness: "Only then will you be able to understand me."

If you have consciousness and silence and meditativeness, there is no need to say that the whole of humanity is one. It is. It is your experience. And it will not be only a brotherhood, it will be a brotherhood and a sisterhood. But that will be just a by-product, there is no need to declare it as a fundamental right.

Article Two: Everyone is entitled to all the rights and freedoms set forth in this declaration without distinction of any kind, such as race, color, sex, language, religion, political or other opinion, national or social origin, property, birth or other status.

All these are bullshit. The first question I was asked as I entered America was that I had to declare under oath that I am not an anarchist—if I am an anarchist, I cannot enter America. Anarchism is a political ideology! I cannot conceive how these people could go on declaring these things. Who is going to ask them, "When are you going to practice them?" Everywhere there is discrimination—in different ways in different countries, but discrimination is there. Mankind needs a great uproar against these so-called humanitarians. They think they are doing a great service. For example in India, for the same amount of work the woman will be paid less. And in this declaration it is said that for the same amount of labor, the same rewards should be paid, whether it is man or woman, white or black does not matter. But it is not true.

In America I was in six jails, and in all the jails there was not a single white man. In six federal jails—which were huge, six hundred people, seven hundred people in one jail . . . but all black people. And you say discrimination is not there? It seems strange—in a white country, all the criminals are black. And that was not all.

I inquired of a few black inmates—because they all loved me; they had been watching me on television for five years, and they had become involved in controversies themselves. They were reading my books, and they were happy that I had come at least for one day to their jail; they would remember this day for their whole lives. I asked them, "What is your crime?"

They said, "All these people you see have not committed any crime. They have been arrested the way you have been arrested, without any arrest warrant. And we have been told again and again: 'You will be taken to the court next week, tomorrow,' but that tomorrow never comes." One man told me that he had been there for nine months without being taken to court.

Now this declaration says nobody should be arrested without an arrest warrant, nobody should be kept in jail unless he is proved a criminal. Innocence needs no proof. You have to prove a person criminal, only then can you keep him in jail. Otherwise you cannot keep him in jail. But people have been there for nine months, eight months, six months in jail—and all young people. So I started figuring out the reason: it is not that they have done anything wrong. The reason is that they are young and revolutionaries. They want rights for the blacks, equal rights for blacks. That is their crime. And they cannot be taken to court because the court will release them, so they are being kept in jail. But this is absolutely criminal on the part of the government of the United States.

I have seen only six jails and near about three or four thousand young black people. Perhaps thousands of people are in other jails. They told me, "Because there is too much pressure from all over the world, that's why they are taking you to court. Otherwise, if the world had remained silent, if the news media had not spread all over the world that the whole government is doing everything criminal against an innocent person . . . The pressure is too much, and the eyes of all the news media are focused on you. They are, under compulsion, reluctantly, taking you to court."

Still, it took them twelve days. That too is against human rights. From the place where I was arrested, the court where I had to be present was only a five hours' flight away. My own jet was there. We offered them our jet. We said, "You can have your pilots; you can have your people, and you can take me to the court. What is the need to keep me here in your jail?"

They would only take me in their own airplane. The whole strategy was: "Today the airplane has not come . . . something is wrong with the airplane"—they had only one airplane, it seems. "The pilot is sick . . ." They took twelve days to make a five hours' journey. But looking at other inmates, I thought, "It is very quick, only twelve days."

Every government goes on doing everything illegal and everything against human rights. And these people are the representatives of governments, and without any shame they can make this declaration—perhaps without even feeling what they are doing. They are lying utterly, white lies.

Article Three: Everyone has the right to life, liberty and security of person.

But death is not included, and it is important. Because birth is not in your hands—you are born without your consent—now only death is there. And you have the choice: either to die without your consent or to die with the dignity of a human being, with your own consent. Not to give death a chance, but to move, yourself, when you have lived enough. But they are worried about putting death into it, because then all the religions and all the political parties will be creating havoc for them. Everything has to be consolatory: "life" . . . but what kind of life?

Just recently in Europe, the Common Market had accumulated mountains of butter and other foodstuffs. In Ethiopia, people were dying of hunger, one thousand people per day, and they had a surplus but they would not give it to Ethiopia. That surplus had to be drowned in the ocean. Just in drowning it, two billion dollars were wasted—that was not the value of the food, it was just the labor of shifting and drowning it in the ocean. And they are doing it every six months, because every six months the surplus is there, and you need more warehouses. And what will you do with it?—fresh crops are coming. But you will not give it to Ethiopia. In India, fifty percent of the people are living below the medical standard of nourishment, and twenty-five percent of the people are almost starving. Fifty percent of people in the villages are eating only one time a day—and when I say eating, don't think of the Taj Mahal Hotel. It means just bread, salt, a little sauce from mangos or from other fruits—that's all. This is not food.

Unless the world is one, we will not be able to give everybody enough nourishment.

And what does it mean to say that you have the right to life? Because people are there, and people are dying; people have died. America is doing the same, Stalin's Russia was doing the same, it is not something happening only in Europe. Every three months America drowns its surplus, and that is worth billions of dollars. In the days of Stalin, Russia was using wheat instead of coal in their railway trains because wheat was cheaper, it was surplus, and coal was difficult and costly to obtain in Russia. People are dying—that is not important. People are starving—that is not important.

Article Nine: No one shall be subjected to arbitrary arrest, detention or exile.

I have been subjected—so I am a witness to it that this declaration is not being followed by any government, and particularly by America, which was the sponsor for this declaration.

I have been in detention in England—not even for an arbitrary reason. I wanted just to stay for six hours at the airport in the first-class lounge because my pilots had flown their time and they wanted to rest. It is against their laws to fly more than twelve hours, so we had to stop. My pilots said, "They may create trouble; they may say that the first-class lounge is for first-class passengers and you are not a passenger; you have your own plane."

Now what class is it, how can they decide? So I told my people to purchase two tickets, two first-class tickets for the morning flight: "We will go with our plane, but purchase two tickets in case they bring up this point"—and they brought up that point. Then we brought up the tickets! The officer was shocked. He had not thought that we would have tickets too. I said, "Now what do you think?"

He said, "I cannot do anything. I will have to ask the higher authorities." And who was the higher authority?

It seems it was the prime minister herself. When the man was gone I looked into his file; he had left it on the table. The government had given him orders. I never asked for any entry visa into England; they should not have bothered. But they decided in Parliament that I should not be allowed in the country—in case I should ask to enter. When the man came back I told him, "I do not want to enter England. Even if the whole of England wants me to enter England, I am the last person to do it. I have no business in England, I just want to sleep in the lounge. And from the lounge you cannot enter the country. It is closed; we will remain only at the airport. And the airport is international, it is not England."

But he said, "What can I do? The insistence is from the top: 'If he insists then put him in detention. That's the only way. He can remain in jail for six hours.'"

I had to remain in jail for six hours—not even for an arbitrary reason. I had not committed any crime, I had the tickets, I had the plane, I just wanted to rest. But the politicians—because I have been exposing them continuously—now have become so frightened that even my sleeping six hours in the lounge at the airport is dangerous for the religion of England, its morality, its character. I can corrupt the youth just by staying in the lounge!

These people are not lovers of human beings. Nor do they have any respect for human dignity.

Article Eighteen: Everyone has the right to freedom of thought, conscience and religion; this right includes freedom to change his religion or belief, and freedom, either alone or in community with others and in public or private, to manifest his religion or belief in teaching, practice, worship and observance.

"Freedom of thought and expression"—I have never done anything except expressing my thoughts. If that is a human right, then no government should have anything against me. I am not active in any politics; I am not interested in any power. I am simply saying whatever I see more clearly than all these blind politicians. What is the fear? "Freedom of expression . . . " The pope has put my books on the black list so that no Catholic should read them. They have a black list. In the Middle Ages, whenever a book appeared on the black list it was burned all over Europe. Now they cannot do that, but this much they can do: "No Catholic should read it." And Catholics are not a small minority—seven hundred million people, a world in itself. Now, preventing them simply means you have accepted defeat; it simply means you don't have any answers to me.

But then why all this nonsense about a Declaration of Human Rights?

Article Nineteen: Everyone has the right to freedom of opinion and expression; this right includes freedom to hold opinions without interference and to seek, receive and impart information and ideas through any media and regardless of frontiers.

This is not right. The Indian parliament has urged Indian journalists and news media people not to give any space to my ideas. The American government has been pressuring the Indian government, so that no news media people from the West should be allowed to take my interview.

The American government has been doing two things: telling all the governments of Europe and Australia that I should not be allowed to reside in their countries, that I should be sent back from everywhere to India. So, all the countries of Europe have passed resolutions in their parliaments that I cannot be allowed in their country even as a tourist for three weeks. The American idea is that I should not be allowed to enter any other country, and nobody who wants to see me or meet me should be allowed to come to India. In this way they feel they can destroy the sannyas movement.

This goes on in reality. Beautiful words and great slogans—but empty.

Article Twenty-Two: Everyone has the right to the free development of his personality.

I don't see that you are allowed to have freedom to develop your personality.

In the first place, the people who wrote this don't know that the personality is the false part of you, and it has not to be developed at all. Your reality is your individuality, which has to be discovered. But they don't talk about individuality. They may not have ever thought of it because they are only personalities, they don't yet have their individuality awake, alert. Naturally, they are writing the word "personality." Personality is an ugly word. It means a mask; the very root of the word is mask. And we don't want people to have masks. People should be natural, spontaneous, themselves.

Article Twenty-Five: All children, whether born in or out of wedlock, shall enjoy the same social protection.

Now, if this is true, it cancels marriage! If a child born from a marriage and a child born outside of marriage have the same rights, then marriage loses all meaning. What is the meaning of marriage? But they don't have the courage to say that. And this too is not true, because nowhere are children born outside marriage respected. They are condemned in every possible way.

I have given this much time to this rubbish because these are the people who are controlling the whole world, and these are the people whose heads should be hammered as much as possible. They have kept humanity in slavery—this should not be allowed any longer.

They don't have any right of declaration. We have the right to declare. We are the people. As far as my people are concerned, we declare that we will live freedom, love, humanity. We will grow into our individuality, and we will help anybody who is inviting and welcoming us.

The only basic right is to become God. And unless you have found God within yourself, everything else is mundane. Finding godliness within you, everything else is found simultaneously.

—

Universal Human Rights for the New Humanity

Osho,
You have spoken to us on the UN Declaration of Human Rights. Would you make your own Declaration of Human Rights for the New Man?

The Declaration of Human Rights basically means that mankind still lives in many kinds of slavery. Otherwise, there would be no need for the declaration. The very need indicates that man has been deceived for thousands of years. And he has been deceived in such a cunning way that unless you rise above humanity, you cannot see in what invisible chains humanity is living, in what bondage, in what invisible prisons everybody is confined.

My declaration of human rights consists of ten fundamental things.

The first is life.

Man has a right to dignity, to health; a right to grow, so that he can blossom into his ultimate flowering. This ultimate flowering is his right. He is born with the seeds, but the society does not provide him the soil, the right caring, the loving atmosphere.

On the contrary, society provides a very poisonous atmosphere, full of anger, hatred, destruction, violence, war. The right to life means there should be no wars anymore. It also means that nobody should be forced into armies, forced to go to war; it is everybody's right to refuse. But this is not the case.

Thousands of people are in prisons—particularly young people, sensitive and intelligent—because they refused to go to war. Their denial has become a crime—and they were simply saying that they don't want to kill human beings. Human beings are not things that you can destroy without a second thought. They are the climax of universal evolution. To destroy them for any cause—for religion, for politics, for socialism, for fascism, it does not matter what the cause is: man is above all causes, and man cannot be sacrificed on any altar.

It is so strange that the UN declares the fundamental rights of human beings and yet says nothing about those thousands of young people who are wasting their lives in prisons for the simple reason that they refused to destroy life. But this has deep roots, which have to be understood.

The right to life is possible only in a certain different atmosphere that is not present on the earth at the moment. Animals are killed, birds are killed, sea animals are killed just for game. You don't have any reverence for life—and life is the same whether it is in human beings or in other forms. Unless man becomes aware of his violence toward the animals, birds, he cannot be really alert about his own right to life. If you are not caring about others' lives, what right do you have to demand the same right for yourself?

People go hunting, killing animals unnecessarily. I was a guest in Maharaja Jamnagar's palace. He showed me hundreds of lions, deer—their heads. The whole palace was full, and he was showing them: "These are the animals I have killed myself."

I asked him, "You look like a nice a person. What was the reason? What have these animals done against you?"

He said, "It is not a question of reason or a question of them doing anything against me. It is just a game."

I said, "Just look from the other side: if a lion killed you, would that be a game? Your wife, your children, your brothers—will any one of them have the guts to say that it was a beautiful game? It will be a disaster! If you kill, then it is a game; if they kill, then it is a calamity. These double standards show your dishonesty, insincerity."

He said, "I have never thought about it."

But the whole of humanity is nonvegetarian; they are all eating other life forms. There is no reverence for life as such. Unless we create an atmosphere of reverence for life, man cannot realize the goal of getting his fundamental right of life.

Secondly, because the UN also declares life to be a fundamental right for man, it is being misused. The pope, Mother Teresa, and their tribe are using it for teaching people against birth control, against abortion, against the pill. Man's mind is so cunning. It was a question of human rights, and they are taking advantage of it. They are saying you cannot use birth control methods because they go against life. The unborn child also has the same right as you have. So some line has to be drawn, because at what point . . . ? To me, the pill does not destroy human rights; in fact it prepares the ground for them. If the earth is too overcrowded, millions of people will die of starvation; there will be wars. And the way the crowd is exploding, it can lead humanity into a very inhuman situation.

In Bengal, there was a great famine in which mothers ate their own children. People sold their own children just for one rupee, two rupees. And do you think the persons who were purchasing them were purchasing human beings? No, they were purchasing food. The pope and Mother Teresa will be responsible for all this.

The pill simply does not allow the child to be formed in the mother's womb, so the question of human rights does not arise. And now, recently, science has found a pill for men, too. It is not necessary that the woman should take the pill, the man can take it. The child is not formed in any way; hence, this fundamental right is inapplicable in that case. But these religious people—the shankaracharyas in India, the ayatollahs in Iran . . . and all over the world, all religions are against birth control methods. And they are the only methods which can prevent man from falling into a barbarous state.

I am absolutely in favor of birth control methods. A child should be recognized as a human being the moment he is born—and then too, I have some reservations. If a child is born blind, if a child is born crippled, if a child is born deaf, dumb, and we cannot do anything . . . Just because life should not be destroyed, this child will have to suffer because of your stupid idea for seventy years, eighty years. Why create unnecessary suffering? If the parents are willing, the child should be put to eternal sleep. And there is no problem in it. Only the body goes back into its basic elements; the soul will fly into another womb. Nothing is destroyed. If you really love the child, you will not want him to live a seventy-year-long life in misery, suffering, sickness, old age. So even if a child is born, if he is not medically capable of enjoying life fully with all the senses, healthy, then it is better that he goes to eternal sleep and is born somewhere else with a better body.

The right to life is a complex thing. Nobody is entitled to kill anyone, either, in the name of religion. Millions of people have been killed in the name of religions, in the service of God. No one should be killed in the name of politics. Again, the same has happened. Joseph Stalin alone killed one million people, his own people, while he was in power. Adolf Hitler killed six million people. And thousands of wars have happened. It seems that on this earth we are doing only one thing: reproducing children because soldiers are needed, reproducing children because wars are needed. It seems man is nothing but a necessary instrument for more destruction, more wars.

The population has to be reduced if man wants to be—to have his dignity, honor, his right to live; not just to drag but to dance. When I say life is a fundamental right, I mean a life of songs and dances, a life of joy and blessings.

My second consideration is for love.

Love should be accepted as one of the most fundamental human rights, and all societies have destroyed it. They have destroyed it by creating marriage. Marriage is a false substitute for love. In the past, small children were married. They had no idea what love is, what marriage is. And why were small children married? For a simple reason: before they become young adults, before love arises in their hearts, the doors have to be closed, because once love takes possession of their hearts then it will become very difficult.

No child marriage is human. A man or a woman should be allowed to choose their partners and to change their partners whenever they feel. The government has no business in it, the society has nothing to do with it. It is two individuals' personal affair. The privacy of it is sacred. If two people want to live together, they don't need any permission from any priest or any government; they need the permission of their hearts. And the day they feel that the time has come to part, again they don't need anybody's permission. They can part as friends, with beautiful memories of their loving days.

Love should be the only way for men and women to live together. No other ritual is needed. The only problem in the past was what would happen to the children; that was the argument for marriage. There are other alternatives, far better. Children should be accepted not as their parents' property—they belong to the whole humanity. From the very beginning it should be made clear to them: "The whole humanity is going to protect you, is your shelter. We may be together—we will look after you. We may not be together; still we look after you. You are our blood, our bones, our souls."

In fact, this possession by the parents of the children is one of the most dangerous things that humanity goes on carrying. This is the root of the idea of possessiveness. You should not possess your children. You can love them, you can bless them, but you cannot possess. They belong to the whole humanity. They come from beyond; you have been just a passage. Don't think more than that about yourself. Whatever you can do, do.

Every commune, every village should take care of the children. Once the commune starts taking care of the children, marriage becomes absolutely obsolete. And marriage is destroying your basic right to love.

If man's love is free, there will not be blacks and whites, and there will not be these ugly discriminations, because love knows no boundaries. You can fall in love with a black man, you can fall in love with a white man. Love knows no religious scriptures. It knows only the heartbeat, and it knows it with absolute certainty. Once love is free, it will prepare the ground for other fundamental rights.

In fact, if you ask the scientists, people falling in love should be as different as possible. Then they will give birth to better children, more intelligent, stronger. We know it now; we are trying it all over the world as far as animals are concerned. Crossbreeding has given us better cows, better horses, better dogs. But man is strange. You know the secret, but you are not bettering yourself. All the royal families are suffering. They create the greatest number of idiots because they go on marrying among themselves. Royal blood cannot mix with a commoner's blood—even in this century we think in terms of royal blood. Blood is simply blood! But if just a dozen families go on marrying among themselves continually, they create many kinds of diseases.

Retardedness is one. Just have a look again at the picture of the Prince of Wales and you will see what I mean by a retarded person. They are fed up, but they cannot go out of their small circle. I have never come across any person belonging to a royal family who has intelligence, and in India I have been acquainted with almost all the royal families. It is not only that their minds remain retarded, their bodies lose many things.

You must have heard the name of Rasputin. Before the Russian revolution he had become the most important man in Russia, for the simple reason that the child of the czar had a disease—if he wounded himself accidentally then the bleeding could not be prevented. No medicine could prevent it, there was no way; the blood would go on flowing out. And that is one of the symptoms of marrying close relatives.

Rasputin was a great hypnotist. He was not a saint and he was not a sinner, he was simply a great hypnotist. He managed with hypnosis to prevent the blood from flowing out of the child. What no physician was able to do . . . and the child was going to be the successor to the greatest empire of those days. Rasputin certainly became very important. Without him the child's life was in danger.

But still those royal families, although they have lost their kingdoms, their empires, continue to marry among themselves. It creates a very weak personality.

There should be no boundaries—that a Hindu should marry only a Hindu, or a brahmin should only marry a brahmin. In fact, the rule should be that the Indian should never marry an Indian. The whole world is there; find your spouse far away, beyond the seven seas, and then you will have children who are more beautiful, more healthy, long living, far more intelligent, geniuses. Man has to learn crossbreeding, but that is possible only if marriage disappears and love is given absolute respect. Right now it is condemned.

The third most fundamental right: death

Because these are the three most important things in life: life, love, and death. Everybody should be given the fundamental right that after a certain age, when he has lived enough and does not want to go on dragging unnecessarily—because tomorrow will be again just a repetition; he has lost all curiosity about tomorrow—he has every right to leave the body. It is his fundamental right. It is his life. If he does not want to continue, nobody should prevent him. In fact, every hospital should have a special ward where people who want to die can enter one month before, can relax, enjoy all the things that they have been thinking about their whole life but could not manage—the music, the literature, if they wanted to paint or sculpt . . . and the doctors should take care to teach them how to relax.

Up to now, death has been almost ugly. Man has been a victim, but it is our fault. Death can be made a celebration; you just have to learn how to welcome it, relaxed, peaceful. And in one month, people, friends, can come to see them and meet together. Every hospital should have special facilities—more facilities for those who are going to die than for those who are going to live. Let them live for one month at least like emperors, so they can leave life with no grudge, with no complaint but only with deep gratitude, thankfulness.

Fourth: the search for truth.

Nobody should be conditioned from childhood about any religion, any philosophy, any theology, because you are destroying his freedom of search. Help him to be strong enough. Help him to be strong enough to doubt, to be skeptical about all that is believed all around him. Help him never to believe, but to insist on knowing. And whatever it takes, however long it takes, to go for the pilgrimage alone, on his own, because there is no other way to find the truth.

All others, who think they are Christians, or they are Jews, or they are Hindus, or they are Muslims—these are all believers. They don't know. Belief is pure poison; knowing is coming to a flowering.

The search for truth . . . you should not teach anybody what truth is because it cannot be taught. You should help the person to inquire. Inquiry is difficult; belief is cheap. But truth is not cheap; truth is the most valuable thing in the world. You cannot get it from others, you will have to find it yourself. And the miracle is, the moment you decide that "I will not fall victim to any belief," you have already traveled half the way toward truth. If your determination is total, you need not go to truth, truth will come to you. You just have to be silent enough to receive it. You have to become a host so that truth can become a guest in your heart.

Right now the whole world is living in beliefs. That's why there is no shine in the eyes, no grace in people's gestures, no strength, no authority in their words. Belief is bogus; it is making castles of sand. A little breeze and your great castle will be destroyed.

Truth is eternal, and to find it means you also become part of eternity.

The fifth basic right: meditation.

To find the truth, all education systems from the kindergarten to the university will create a certain atmosphere for meditation. Meditation does not belong to any religion, and meditation is not a belief. It is a pure science of the inner. Learning to be silent, learning to be watchful, learning to be a witness; learning that you are not the mind, but something beyond—the consciousness—will prepare you to receive truth.

And it is truth that has been called by many people "God," by others "nirvana," by others, other names have been given to it, but it is a nameless silence, serenity, peace. The peace is so deep that you disappear, and the moment you disappear you have entered the temple of God.

But strange it is, that people are wasting almost one-third of their lives in schools, colleges, and universities, not knowing anything about silence, not knowing anything about relaxation, not knowing anything about themselves. They know about the whole world—it is very weird that they have forgotten only themselves. But it seems there is some reason. . . .

In India there is an ancient story. Ten blind men pass through a stream. The current is very forceful, so they hold hands. Reaching the other side, somebody suggests, "We should count ourselves. The current was so forceful and we cannot see—somebody may have gone with the wind, gone with the river." So they count. Strangely enough, the counting always stops at nine. Everybody tries, but it is always nine. One man sitting on the bank of the river starts laughing—it is hilarious! And those ten blind people are sitting there crying, tears in their eyes because they have lost one of their friends.

The man comes to them and he says, "What is the matter?"

They explain the situation. He says, "You all stand up in a line. I will hit the first person—he has to say 'one.' I will hit the second person—he has to say 'two,' because I will hit twice. I will hit the third person three times; he has to say 'three.'" Strangely enough, he finds the tenth man who was lost!

They all thank him, they touch his feet; they say, "You are a god to us. We were thinking we had lost one of our friends. But please, can you tell us . . . we were also counting; all of us tried, and the tenth was not there. How has he appeared suddenly?"

The man says, "That is an ancient mystery which you will not understand. Just go on your way."

What is the ancient mystery in it? One tends to forget oneself. In fact, one lives his whole life without remembering himself. He sees everybody, he knows everybody else, he just forgets himself.

Meditation is the only method in which you will start counting from yourself: "one." And because it is not part of any religion, there is no problem—it should be all over the world, in every school, in every college, in every university. Anybody who comes home from the university should come with a deep, meditative being, with an aura of meditation around him. Otherwise, what he is bringing is all rubbish, crap. Geography he knows: he knows where Timbuktu is, he knows where Istanbul is, and he does not know where he is himself.

The first thing in life is to know who you are, where you are. Then everything in your life starts settling, moving in the right direction.

The sixth: freedom in all dimensions.

We are not even as free as birds and animals. No bird goes to the passport office. Any moment he can fly into Pakistan; no entry visa. Strange, that only man remains confined in nations, in boundaries. Because the nation is big, you tend to forget that you are imprisoned. You cannot get out of it, you cannot get into it. It is a big prison, and the whole earth is full of big prisons. Freedom in all dimensions means that man, wherever he is born, is part of one humanity.

Nations should dissolve, religions should dissolve, because they are all creating bondages—and sometimes very hilarious bondages.

I was in Devas, an Indian city. For twenty years the Jaina temple there had not opened. There were three locks on the temple: one lock from the Digambaras, one of the sects of Jainism, one from another sect, Svetambaras, and the third from the police. For twenty years poor Mahavira had been inside—no food, no bath, no light. One wonders whether he was really alive or dead because he did not make any noise . . . at least he could knock and shout, "Open the doors and let me out!"

When I saw it, I asked, "What is the matter?" I was just passing by, and I saw three locks—big locks, bigger than you may have ever seen—and I came to know the story.

In Devas, there is only one Jaina temple, and this was the temple. Jainas are few; they don't have enough money to make two temples, so they have made one temple and divided the time. Up to twelve o'clock in the morning, Digambaras will worship, and after twelve, Svetambaras will worship . . . but there was a fight every day.

The differences between Svetambaras and Digambaras are not very big—so childish and so stupid! Digambaras worship Mahavira with closed eyes, and Svetambaras worship Mahavira with open eyes. This is the only basic difference. Now a marble statue . . . either you can make the eyes closed or you can make the eyes open, unless you fix some mechanism to switch on so he opens his eyes, and switch off so he closes them. But that much technology does not exist in India; otherwise it would not be difficult. You can find it in toys—a beautiful doll, you lie her down and she closes her eyes. You put her back and she opens her eyes. Something could have been arranged.

But they had something arranged—primitive, but they had arranged it. And it is being followed all over India: when Svetambaras worship a statue which has closed eyes, they put false eyelids on top; they just glue them on. That is simple, nontechnical; not much technology is needed. But every day the problem was there: at the time of twelve, exactly twelve, Svetambaras would be waiting. One minute more . . . the Digambaras are worshipping, and they are worshipping knowingly a little longer—and the Svetambaras will come and start putting their eyes on the statue, and the fight will start.

It happened so many times that finally the police locked the temple and said to them, "Go to the court and get a decision." The case goes on—how can the court decide whether Mahavira used to meditate with closed eyes or with open eyes? The reality is, he used to meditate with half open eyes.

No child should be given any idea by the parents what life is all about—no theology, no philosophy, no politics. He should be made as intelligent and sharp as possible, so when he comes of age he can go in search. And it is a lifelong search. People today get their religion when they are born. In fact, if you can get your religion when you die, you have found it early. It is such a precious treasure, but it is possible only out of freedom—and freedom in all dimensions, not only in religion.

There should be no nations, no national boundaries. There should be no religions. Man should be taken as man. Why confine him with so many adjectives? Right now he is not free in any way.

I was arrested in America. In one jail in Oklahoma, the US Marshal told me that I had to write my name as David Washington. I said, "This is the first time that somebody has told me my name. Do you read thoughts?"

He became a little puzzled. He said, "Is it really your name?"

I said, "Of course."

He said, "Then change it. Some other name will do."

But I said, "You know my name. David Washington is not my name; why should I write David Washington? And you call this country a democracy! And not even the freedom to write one's own name. What other freedoms do you have? And on your coat there is written in big letters 'Department of Justice, US Marshal.'" I said, "At least take this coat off. David Washington is not my name, and I am not going to write it." I said, "This is for the first time in my life that I am seeing how democracy works, how freedom works. I am not even free to write my name. What is the purpose?"

He said, "That, I don't know. From high above I have been ordered: `David Washington should be his name, and he should be called David Washington in jail.'"

I said, "Then you fill out the form"—and it was in the middle of the night, twelve o'clock. I said, "You fill out the form—I will not fill it out, I refuse—and then I will sign it."

He was in a hurry to go home, so he filled out the form. I signed my name. He looked at it and he said, "But it doesn't look like David Washington."

I said, "How can it? I don't look like David Washington."

He said, "You are a strange man. You deceived me."

I said, "You are deceiving yourself. You know perfectly well what my name is. And tomorrow the whole world will know that the so-called democracies—free countries, talking so much of freedom – are not even able to allow people to write their own names." And I said, "You don't know the reason your higher authorities have asked this?"

He said, "I don't know."

I said, "This is strange, because I know. It is a simple, logical inference that even if you kill me in the jail, nobody will be able to find out where I disappeared. Because in your forms, on your register, I never entered your jail, so the question of my being killed in your jail does not arise."

He was shocked. I said, "This is a simple thing. Otherwise, there is no need to change my name; you don't have any authority."

But in this world there is no freedom in any dimension.

I was going to college. My parents wanted me to go to science college or to medical college. I said, "Am I going, or are you going?"

They said, "Of course you are going; why should we be going?"

"Then," I said, "leave it to me."

They said, "We can leave it to you, but then remember: we will not support you financially."

I said, "That's understood." I left my home without a single rupee. I traveled in the train to the university without a ticket. I had to go to the ticket checker and tell him, "This is the situation. Can you allow me to travel without a ticket?"

He said, "This is the first time in my life that somebody has come to ask me! People escape, people deceive me, cheat me. Certainly I will take you, and at the university station I will be at the gate so nobody bothers you."

I went directly to the vice-chancellor and told him the whole story. And I told him, "I want to study philosophy, but it seems there is no freedom even to choose what I want to study. So you have to give me all the scholarships possible, because I will not be getting any financial help. Otherwise I will study philosophy fasting . . . even if I die."

He said, "No! Don't do that because then the blame will be on me. I will give you all the scholarships."

From the very childhood we go on crippling, cutting freedoms; we try to make a child according to our desires.

I was talking to a Christian missionary and he said, "God made man in his own image."

I said, "That is the foundation of all slavery. Why should God make man in his own image? Who is he?—and to give his own image to man means he has destroyed man from the very beginning." And that is what every father is doing.

Man's basic right is to be himself.

And in an authentic human society, everybody should be allowed to be himself—even if he chooses just to be a flute player and he will not become the richest man in the world, but will be a beggar on the streets. Still I say freedom is so valuable. You may not be the president of the country, you may be just a beggar playing the flute in the streets. But you are yourself, and there is such deep contentment, fulfillment, that unless you know it you have missed the train.

Seventh: one earth, one humanity

I don't see any reason at all why there should be so many nations. Why should there be so many lines on the map? They are only on the map, remember—they are not on the earth; neither are they in the sky. And the map is man-made. Existence has not created this earth in fragments.

I am reminded of one of my teachers. He was a very loving human being, and he had his own methods of teaching. He was a kind of rebel. One day he came with a few pieces of cardboard, placed them on the table, and said to us all, "Look, this is the map of the world, but I have cut it into pieces and I have mixed them. Now anybody who is confident that he can put them in their right places and make the world map should come up."

One tried, failed; another tried, failed. I went on watching him and watching the people who were failing and why they were failing. Watching five persons fail, I was the sixth. I went and I turned over all his cardboard pieces. He said, "What are you doing?"

I said, "You wait, I am working it out. Five people have failed, but I have found the secret."

On the other side of the map was a picture of a man. I arranged the man, which was easier. On one side the man was arranged, and on the other side the whole map of the world was arranged. That was the key that I had been looking for, waiting to see if I could get some clue. And when the others were arranging the pieces, I saw that there was something on the other side.

The teacher said, "You are a rascal! I was hoping you would come first, but when you didn't come I understood that you were waiting to find out the key. And you have found the right key."

The world is divided because man is divided. Man is divided because the world is divided.

Start from anywhere; just let the whole of humanity be one, and the nations will disappear, the lines will disappear. It is our world—one humanity, one earth, and we can make it a paradise. Right now there is no need to describe hell. You can just look all around; it is here.

I have heard a story. A man died. He was a thief, a murderer, a rapist—you name it, and he had done it. And when the angels started taking him away, he said, "Certainly you will be taking me to hell."

They said, "No."

He said, "What?"

They said, "You have been in hell; now we are taking you to heaven. The old hell is empty because you have created a better hell, so all the sinners are sent here." And the story seems to be significant. Looking around the earth, man is in such misery and suffering that there seems to be no need for another hell.

But we can change the whole situation. This earth can become a paradise. And then there will be no need for any paradise; paradise will be empty.

Eighth: uniqueness of every individual.

A very beautiful word has been misused so utterly that it is difficult to imagine, and that word is "equality." A few thinkers say human beings are equal. And the United Nations declares that equality is man's birthright. But nobody bothers to see that man is not equal and has never been equal. It is absolutely un-psychological.

Every human being is unique. The moment you are all equal, you are a crowd. Your individuality has been taken away. You are no longer yourself, but just a cog in the wheel.

I teach not equality, not inequality—I teach uniqueness. Every individual is unique and needs to be respected in his uniqueness. Because every individual is unique, the birthright should be equal opportunity for their growth of uniqueness.

It is such a simple and obvious fact. Two thousand years have passed, and you have not been able to produce another Jesus. Twenty-five centuries have passed, and you have not been able to produce another Gautam Buddha. And still you go on saying people are equal? Each person is unique, and everybody should be respected as a world in himself or herself. One is neither inferior to anybody nor is one superior to anybody; each is alone.

In this aloneness there is beauty. You are no longer a mob, a crowd. You are yourself.

Ninth: a world government.

I am absolutely against governments. I am for one government for the whole world. That means no war will be possible; that means there will be no need to keep millions of people in armies unnecessarily. They can be productive, they can be helpful, and if they are merged into humanity, all poverty will disappear.

Right now seventy percent of the national income of every country goes to the army, and the rest of the country lives on thirty percent. If armies disappear, seventy percent of the income of every country will be available. There is no need to be poor, there is no need to have any beggars. These beggars, these Ethiopias, they are our creations. On the one hand we are creating great armies, and on the other hand we are killing human beings through starvation. And these armies are doing nothing! They are simply professional killers, professional criminals, trained criminals. We are giving them training in how to kill. We talk about humanity, we talk about civilization, and still seventy percent of our income goes into killing.

One world government means a tremendous change, a revolution. The whole earth will be benefited by it.

Secondly, if there is one world government it becomes only functional. Right now government is not functional, it has real power. The president of a country or the prime minister of a country . . . in a functional government things will be different. Now you have the postmaster general; he is a functional person, he has no power. He has work, he has a function, but he has no power. There is no need. The man who heads your railways, what power does he have? The man who is the president of your airlines, what power does he have? It is functional.

If there is only one government, it will automatically become functional. Right now it cannot be because the fear of other governments keeps you afraid: "Make your leaders strong, give all support to the leaders." But if there is no war, there is no need of anybody having power—war is the cause of power. And unless war disappears from the world, power cannot disappear; they are together.

A functional world government—like the post office, the railways, the airlines—will be efficient but without power. It will be a beautiful world where you don't know who the president is, who the prime minister is—they are your servants. Right now they have become your masters, and to keep their power they have to keep you always completely afraid. Pakistan is getting ready to fight with India, so you have to give all power to the Indian leaders. China is going to attack . . .

Adolf Hitler has written in his autobiography that if you want to remain in power, keep people always afraid. And he is absolutely right. Sometimes mad people are also right.

And tenth: meritocracy.

Democracy has failed.

We have lived under many kinds of governments—aristocracy, monarchy, city democracies—and now we have seen the whole world getting addicted to the idea of democracy. But democracy has not solved any problems; it has increased the problems. It was because of these problems that a man like Karl Marx supported a dictatorship of the proletariat. I am not a supporter of a dictatorship of the proletariat, but I have another idea that goes far ahead of democracy.

Democracy means government by the people, of the people, for the people—but it is only in words. In India right now there are nine hundred million people. How can nine hundred million people have power? They have to delegate the power to somebody. So it is not the people who rule, but those who are chosen by the people. What are your grounds for choosing? How do you manage to choose? And are you capable of choosing the right people? Have you been trained, educated for a democratic life?

No, nothing has been done. The ignorant masses can be exploited very easily by very insignificant things. For example, Nixon lost his election against Kennedy, and the only reason was that Kennedy looked better on television than Nixon; this is the analysis of the psychoanalysts. Nixon improved: when he discovered this, before the next election he improved; he learned how to stand, how to walk, how to talk, how to dress. Even the color of your clothing will make a difference on television. If you go there in white clothes you will look like a ghost. Arbitrary reasons . . . somebody speaks well, is a good orator. But that does not mean that he will make a good president. Somebody makes good shoes—do you think that will make him a good president?

It happened when Abraham Lincoln was chosen president. On the day of his inaugural address to the Senate, people were feeling very angry and hurt—because Lincoln's father was a shoemaker, and a shoemaker's son has defeated the great aristocrats. They were offended. One arrogant aristocrat could not tolerate it. Before Lincoln started speaking, he said, "Wait a minute. Do you recognize me? You used to come with your father to my house sometimes because your father made shoes for my family. You used to help him." And the whole Senate laughed. This was an effort to humiliate Lincoln.

But you cannot humiliate people like Abraham Lincoln. He said, "I am very grateful to you that you reminded me of my dead father at this moment. Because my father was the best shoemaker in the whole country, and I know that I can never be the best president as he was the best shoemaker. He is still ahead of me."

What criterion do you use? How do you manage?

That's why my idea is that the days of democracy are over. A new kind of system is needed, based on merit. We have thousands of universities all over the world. Why have ordinary, unknowledgeable, ignorant masses chosen people who will be holding tremendous power for five years in their hands? And now the power is so great that they can destroy the whole world. Meritocracy means that only people who are educated in a certain area should be able to vote in that area. For example, only the educationists of the country should choose the education minister. Then you will have the best education minister possible. For the finance minister, you should choose some-body who knows finance, somebody who knows the complexities of economics. But this choice is possible only for people who are trained in economics, in financial matters—and there are thousands of people. For every post, the person who is chosen should be chosen by experts. The health minister should be chosen by all the doctors, the surgeons, the medical experts, the scientists who are working in the medical field. Then we will have the cream of our genius, and we can depend on this cream to make the life of all humanity more peaceful, more blissful, more rich.

This idea I call a meritocracy. And once you have chosen all the people, then these people can choose the president and the prime minister. They will be our geniuses; they can choose the prime minister, the president from the country, or they can choose from the members of the parliament. And for the parliament we should also make gradations.

For example, people who have at least a postgraduate degree should be able to vote. Just becoming twenty-one years old does not mean you are able to choose the right person. At twenty-one years, you don't know anything about life and its complexities. At least a postgraduate degree should be held by those who choose the members of the parliament or the senate or whatever you call it. In this way, we can make an educated, refined, cultured government. Before the world government happens, each nation should pass through a meritocracy. And once we have enjoyed the fruits of a meritocracy, then these people will be able to understand that if we can combine the whole world into one government, life can certainly be a joy, worth living—not to renounce, but to rejoice.

Up to now, whatever has happened has been accidental. Our history up to now is nothing but a history of accidents. We have to stop this. Now we have to decide that the future is not going to be accidental. It will be created by us; and to create our world can be the greatest creation possible.

—

The UN and the "Scourge of War"

Osho,
On the fortieth anniversary of the UN, the one-cent American postal stamp has the message, "We the peoples of the United Nations determine to save succeeding generations from the scourge of war." Can the UN save humanity from war?

The UN has proved in these forty years only one thing: that it is as impotent as its predecessor, the League of Nations.

The members of the UN are the people who are going to create the third world war. The UN has no power to prevent it; it is only a debating club, and not of the best kind. It is not even democratic—the big powers like America and Russia have the capacity to veto any resolution. Just one nation, America or Russia, can stop any resolution which is being passed by the whole world. Is this democratic?

Every nation, small or big, poor or rich, must have equal rights! In forty years the UN has not been able even to do that. It is just keeping people consoled: "Don't be afraid, we are going to save you." In fact, from whom are they going to save us? They are the people we have to be saved from!

The UN has not been able to stop the increasing amount of nuclear weapons. That should be the first step if you don't want the third world war. Why wait for the last moment? Why not start it now? And the basic step will be that no war preparations are made. When everybody is prepared to fight . . . in fact they will be forced to fight, just because each country has invested so much energy and power, and it has piled up nuclear weapons sky high: what are the nations going to do with those weapons? And they have poured such immense amounts of money into them. At what point will the UN stop them? And Russia can just veto it, America can veto it.

But this is how politicians have been cheating humanity all along, throughout the whole history of man. They say one thing and they do just the opposite. It is very easy to publish a postal stamp that says, "We the peoples of the United Nations are determined to save humanity from the scourge of war." Who are these "we"? Have you asked the people of the world?

Nobody wants war around the world except these idiotic politicians, because without war they have no job. War keeps politicians powerful. People have to depend on politicians because the war is coming.

Adolf Hitler wrote in his autobiography, *My Struggle* . . . he has a few very important points to make. The first thing he says is that never in history has a great leader been born unless there is war. That's true. If there had been no Second World War, you would have never heard of Adolf Hitler, Benito Mussolini, Winston Churchill, Roosevelt—they all became stars, high in the sky. Of course, millions of people died to make them great leaders of men.

The same has been the case all along, throughout history. The politician wants to be on the top, as high as possible. If there is peace, no fight, no war, no preparation for war, he is just ordinary—perhaps a little bit less intelligent than the average person. His intelligence is not better than the average person's; it can be worse.

Before the Second World War, the same promise was given by the League of Nations: "We are going to save the world from war." But those were the same people who fought the Second World War. And I say to you, these same people who constitute the UN are going to create the third world war.

These stamps are cheap. You can go on befooling humanity, but for how long? It is time that humanity understands the politician and his cunningness. Even in the UN you cannot be peaceful, discussing in a friendly way. I said it is only a debating club and not the best one, because nobody is listening to anybody else. It is a tower of Babel: everybody is speaking for his government, his nation, his politics, and is not ready to listen to anything else.

Do you know what Khrushchev did in the UN? He was the premier of the Soviet Union. This kind of behavior, and the people who behave in this way—can they prevent the third world war? Then who is going to start it? Do they think I am going to start the third world war? That the sannyasins around the world are going to start the third world war? Khrushchev was delivering his talk to the UN, and he became so angry that he took his shoe off and started beating on the table with the shoe! A great history of forty years— not an ordinary history. They could not prevent even Khrushchev beating their faces with his shoe, shouting and screaming at the whole UN.

In forty years they have not been able to do anything at all, this is a sheer wastage of time. The fortieth anniversary should be declared as the death of the UN, finished! There is no point, they cannot agree. But the existence of UN gives consolation to people: "We don't need to be worried, the UN is taking care of us." And the UN consists of warring nations who have nuclear weapons. They have been talking about putting a stop to it, but it is just pure talk; nobody stops.

I think it is time that the people of the world start understanding the politician and his hypocrisy, his double personality, because if the third world war happens, then there will be no life on this beautiful planet.

I don't believe at all in this Declaration of the UN, but I have another program for the people:

First, don't trust your politicians. Don't be consoled by their cunning strategies.

Second, remember that you are going to be destroyed with your children, with your wife, with your parents, with your trees, with your animals—everything that is alive on the earth.

If the people of the whole earth simply refuse and say, "We are not going to fight, there is no point in it." If they refuse and say, "We don't want boundaries of nations."

If there is going to be no war, why keep these boundaries? What purpose do these boundaries serve? If the people of the world force their governments and say, "Disperse all your armies. Let those people be creative. . . ."

Millions of people around the earth, in the army, are just doing nothing. In fact, they are hankering for war. They are not meditators who can just sit silently, doing nothing and the grass grows by itself. They are very ordinary people. To keep them holding their guns, watching their nuclear missiles—how long can you keep them in this situation? Sooner or later, they will find it is better now to start: "We are tired, and bored." This is an established fact, that during the war people are less sad, more excited, happier than they are in peaceful times, because so much is going on. Every moment brings new news; excitement is natural.

Human history can be divided in two parts: first when there is war, second when they are preparing for a new war. There has never been a period of real peace. Preparing for war is cold war—getting ready, because the last war has taken so much, destroyed so much that you have to prepare again. Within ten to twenty years' time they are again ready. The weapons are ready, the enemies are there.

If they really mean what they say, then take the preliminary steps: The first is to dissolve boundaries, dissolve passports and green cards. The world, the whole earth is ours. Wherever we want to be, it is nobody's business to prevent us. Let there be freedom of movement. Let all the races, all the nations get mixed. And once the boundaries are not there, they will get mixed, they will spread all over the world—all kinds of races—and it will be a great experiment in crossbreeding. We will have better generations to come.

It is not enough to save the coming generations from war if they are simply carbon copies of you. What is the point? If they are carbon copies of you, they will do the same as you have been doing. A New Man is needed, a New Man who feels the whole earth is his mother – not small segments of it. Do you see? You call your land your motherland, and you have cut the mother into so many pieces—is your mother alive still? You are carrying only limbs of your mother. Somebody has taken the leg, somebody has taken the head . . . .

I am reminded of a religious master. He had two disciples, just as every democracy has two political parties. Those disciples were competing in every way to get more attention from the master. And the question basically was, who was going to succeed the master—he was getting old. So both were trying their best to serve the master, to follow the master, to practice the discipline that the master has given. But the motivation was neither the discipline nor the principles; they were not concerned with the master at all.

One summer day the master was sleeping, and they were not going to lose any opportunity. So they were both massaging the legs of the master. He was tired, naturally—he had come from a long journey. One was working on the left leg, the other was working on the right leg. The master was asleep. The man who was working on the right leg told the other, "Remember, if your leg comes on top of my leg, I am not going to tolerate it." The other said, "And what do you think?—I am going to tolerate it? I will cut off your leg if it comes on my leg!" And they both had their swords ready.

The master was not really asleep, no master ever is. He opened his eyes and said, "Boys, those legs are both mine! Who told you that the right leg is owned by one, and the left leg is owned by the other?"

But this is the situation of the world. The mother earth has been cut into thousands of pieces. People have to be awakened to the fact. To stop calling America your motherland, stop calling Germany your fatherland. You see the difference? The whole world calls its country the motherland, except Germany: their land is the fatherland. It is not a coincidence, they are more male chauvinistic than anybody else.

Stop all this nonsense!—and people can do it. I am preparing you to spread the fire around the world that the whole earth belongs to us. And let the UN go on discussing. If they want to wrestle against each other in the UN building, they can have good boxing matches. It is better than throwing shoes at each other. And it will be really great entertainment, seeing your great politicians wrestling! But that will not be decisive as far as the earth is concerned.

The people of the earth have to take the responsibility from the hands of the politicians. And this will be a first step: to erase all the boundaries. And see how many people they can put in jail; you cannot put a whole nation in jail.

All the constitutions of democratic countries accept in their list of birthrights the right of movement. But where is it? You can move only within the country. They have given you a little rope to feel that you are free, but an authentic freedom of movement will mean that anybody can go anywhere on the earth. Wherever he feels to live, he can live; no hindrance should be there. Removal of the boundaries will bring one world, and one world functional government.

The UN has no power over anything. I know it . . . . In India, in 1947 after independence, Pakistan invaded Kashmir, which was part of India, and took over a large chunk of land. India fought against Pakistan. It could have been the beginning of a third world war, because the land that Pakistan had taken was very significant; it joined Pakistan with China.

Pakistan now could have a road—now they do have a road—going over the Himalayas to Peking. And China is not on speaking terms with Russia anymore. China is going to be with America, so that small piece of land is of immense significance.

And what did the UN do? It did not force Pakistan, because America would not like that land to be lost, it is a key point in any war in Asia. So the UN did something futile. They said, "First stop the war, have a ceasefire line." On one side Indian armies have been standing for forty years, on the other side Pakistani armies have been standing for forty years. Between the two is the camp of the UN observers to make sure that the cease-fire line is not crossed till the matter is settled. Who is going to settle it? And if you cannot settle such a small matter in forty years, how many centuries will you take to settle the third world war?

They cannot settle the matter because if they settle in favor of Pakistan, Russia will veto it; the settlement is finished. If they settle it in favor of India, America will veto it, and the matter is finished. So it is in limbo, and it is going to be in limbo perhaps forever, unless my people succeed in dissolving all boundaries; then that cease-fire line will also dissolve.

And this is a sheer wastage!—thousands of people unnecessarily standing there with their guns ready, on alert, on both sides. Just a single crackpot can start shooting, just out of boredom. Forty years . . . ! He was young, now he is old, getting senile. Just for the sake of fun, if one man starts firing from the other side, then immediately both the armies will jump up, and nobody will care about the observers. Perhaps they will be the first ones to be killed.

What has the UN to its credit? Nothing at all. Without any credibility, to claim that they are going to stop the third world war is simply befooling the people. They cannot stop the war between India and Pakistan, between Pakistan and Bangladesh. They cannot stop the war between Israel and the surrounding Muslim countries, because everywhere these two great powers are involved. Israel is supported by the Americans, because the American political parties cannot survive without the Jews' donations to their parties. If they want donations from Jews, they have to stand by the side of Israel. And Russia is behind the Muslim countries, which are bigger, surrounding the small Israel from all sides. And since the birth of Israel, the child has been in bed, almost dead, but America is keeping it alive by artificial breathing. If America steps out, Israel will be finished within a day.

America cannot step out, Russia cannot step out. In fact, it is a good opportunity; America has created it. They have the vast majority of Muslim countries of the whole Middle East sympathetic toward them, because in any case these countries will need support. They are all oil countries, that's why America is hesitating, is now in a fix: if it does too much, goes a little more toward support of Israel, then all the oil countries are in the hands of Soviet Russia. And oil is now far more precious than gold.

The UN in forty years has not been able to do anything—and still these people have the nerve to say they are going to save the world from a third world war. Even in small wars they have not been able: what did the UN do in Vietnam? Poor people were being killed unnecessarily by the Americans. It was none of America's business. Vietnam belongs to the people who live there, and if they want to be communist, who are you to prevent them? What right have you got? The same was the situation in Korea. The UN has failed utterly, and I am amazed that they are not even ashamed, and are declaring that they will save the coming generations from the third world war.

Only one thing can save the world from the coming war—which will be a total war, for the first time; all other wars were child's play. This is going to destroy the whole of life on the earth. Trees, birds, animals, man—anything living will simply be gone. I say there is one way only, and that is to spread to people more meditativeness, more love, more friendliness, more rejoicing.

If we can make the earth sing songs and dance in joy, in gratitude because existence has given so much—otherwise, it would have been impossible even to purchase one sunrise! The whole wealth of the earth would not be able to purchase one sunrise. And a sunrise is a big thing—the whole wealth of the earth would not be able to produce a single rose flower, and all this is given to man without his asking.

You don't deserve it, you are not worthy of it! It is out of the compassion of existence, the overflowing joy of existence, the continuous creativity of existence that you are so rich. Millions of stars in the night. . . Make people aware of their gratitude toward life, and make people love, sing, dance. If we can spread this at-ease-ness around the world, the third world war will be prevented. We need not bother about it. Joyous people don't want war.

It is only those who are already dead who would like everybody else to be dead. They are really suffering because they are dead. They cannot laugh, they cannot enjoy, they cannot love, they cannot feel. They don't have any heart, and others have—it is making them so jealous, it will be far better that everything is finished. At least there will be no grounds for their jealousy; they will also be finished in it!

So I don't say that there is any direct way to prevent the third world war. That is what the pacifists of the world say: "Protest. Have protest marches to Washington, to Moscow"—but nobody listens to those protest marches, and I have seen those pacifists shouting and screaming against the war. I could not see any difference between them and the people who are getting ready to fight; their screaming was enough proof that they belonged to the same category. If those pacifists had weapons and missiles, they would create a war to prevent the third world war—the way they are shouting and screaming and throwing stones simply shows that they are of the same species as the politicians against whom they are throwing stones. The difference is just that the politicians have the power, and they don't have the power.

Remember, the husband does not scream at the wife, the wife screams at the husband. When he gets tired of her nagging and screaming, he hits the wife, he beats her. And strangely, the wife simply becomes silent. If she is not beaten, then she is going to drive the man nuts. In old countries like India and China, it was told to the newly-married couple by their elders—the husband was told, "Remember, once in a while a wife needs beating; otherwise, you will not be able to live peacefully."

But why does the wife scream?—because the husband has the muscular strength, she cannot beat the husband. There are a few exceptions, but exceptions only prove the rule. She would like to beat him, but as far as muscular strength is concerned, she cannot compete with the husband. So the moment the husband starts beating her, she becomes peaceful.

The weak, the powerless, scream. The powerful takes his gun, puts his army on alert. The pacifists continually go on protesting. This helps nobody. Nobody listens to their protest.

I used to know a man. . . . My house in one city was just near

the high court of the state, so all protest marches, all kinds of pacifists were passing in front of my door. And I watched them—their
behavior did not seem to be peaceful. They looked more ugly than
the people in the high court. But I was amazed that one man was
always there, whether the communist party was protesting, or the
socialist party was protesting, or the people's party was protesting.
And in India there are so many parties. He was always there, with
every party.

One day I got hold of him, and I asked him, "You are an amazing
man—to what party do you belong?"

He said, "Who cares? I am a member of all the parties."

I said, "But how it is possible? Communists are against the
socialists, socialists are against the communists. How can you be?"

He said, "I am not concerned with their politics—I enjoy screaming!
It is such a healthy thing that whenever there is a protest I close my
shop; and whoever is protesting, I am always ahead holding the
flag." He said, "It is really healthy."

I said, "I know. My people are doing it every morning, but they
don't protest about anybody." I said to him, "It is better that you start
Dynamic Meditation, because these protests happen only once in a
while, and you have to be dependent on these political parties.
There is no need, you can do it on your own."

He said, "On my own? Alone?"

"No," I said, "don't be worried" . . . I had a meditation hall there.
I said, "Every morning many people come there." And he started
coming. Now he is a sannyasin, I don't think for any other reason,
just every day, early in the morning, it is healthy to scream! It gives
you stronger lungs, a better heart, more strength. And moreover, he
need not close his shop anymore; financially it is good.

I am not a pacifist, and I don't want my people to be pacifists.
That is fighting with those who are preparing for war, but you are
doing the same on a small scale, in a feminine way. No, that won't
help. We want to create our own movement which has nothing to do
with the third world war.

Do you see my point? If we can make humanity happier, more
loving, more silent, more peaceful, we will create a real barrier
against the third world war. The leaders cannot go without their
people. If the people refuse, the armies refuse, if everybody refuses
and says, "I am so happy, I don't want to die. And I love humanity,

so I don't want to kill. If you can manage on your own, you do it."

A peaceful and happy man does not want to die and does not want to kill.

—

Starting Over: Roadmaps for a
Revolution in Consciousness

There are no people who have never dreamed of a beautiful future and who have never been in a state of innocence, who have never tasted something of peace, something of love, something of beauty. But all this has been destroyed, distorted, contaminated, poisoned by an ugly society.

Its only power is in its ancientness. But now that very power, that ancientness, is going to prove its greatest weakness. It just needs a little push. It is a dead society already; it has prepared its grave with its own hands, and it is standing just on the corner of the grave. You just have to push. . . .

We have to start from scratch. Again Adam and Eve, again the Garden of Eden...again the very beginning.

Bravo America?

Osho,
George Gurdjieff's last words to his disciples were, "Bravo,
America." I have heard you appreciated his insight about
America, but right now the way American bureaucracy and
politicians are behaving, it seems the words of Gurdjieff are no
longer relevant.

No, they are still relevant. A man like George Gurdjieff never
becomes irrelevant. People of that category are eternally relevant.
Politicians may be behaving in an ugly way—the only way they
know—but America is not just the American politicians.

Gurdjieff's last words before he died were, "Bravo, America." His
disciples were at a loss to figure it out. Their whole life they had
been in trouble with this man, and now, at the last . . . . Nobody
could have expected that his dying words would be, "Bravo,
America." And he was dying in France! And now he is dead, so you
cannot even ask, "What do you mean?" But what he said was more
significant, meaningful, than ordinary intellect can understand.

America is the youngest country in the whole world. Its history is
only three hundred years; it is nothing compared to the histories of
China, India. In India, three hundred years mean nothing. The Indian
astrologers prove—and nobody has been able to contradict them
yet—that Indian civilization is at least ninety thousand years old. In
the Rigveda, the most ancient book in the whole world, a certain
constellation of stars is described in detail, in every particular, precisely. That constellation happened ninety thousand years ago,
according to the scientists. Since then, that kind of configuration has

not happened again. There is no way for the people who were writing the Rigveda to describe the stars and their constellations in such precise and exact detail unless they had observed it. Now the proof is such that no argument can defeat it. A country which is ninety thousand years old—what does three hundred years mean to it? China perhaps is even older.

Gurdjieff's statement means first that America has no burden of past conditioning—one thing. It is a very thin layer of conditioning, three hundred years, in comparison to ninety thousand years. To change the Hindu mind is almost impossible. It is so old, so thick; so deep have gone the roots. But the American mind is only very superficially conditioned—one thing which makes it possible that America can be deprogrammed, and Americans can become the first citizens of a new world. Perhaps Gurdjieff was remembering the words "brave new world" when he said, "Bravo, America."

Secondly, America is the only country where all kinds of people—Spanish, Italian, English, German, Swedish, Belgian, Swiss—all kinds of people have mixed. It is not a race; it is more cosmopolitan than any other country. The man of the future has to be cosmopolitan. He cannot be an Italian, a German, an Indian, an African. No, he can only be a human being. There is more possibility in America for it to happen. All other countries are racial; America is a nonracial country; it is a tremendous opportunity to create a new world without any racial mind.

Thirdly, America is more receptive to new ideas, new technologies, new scientific research than any other country, for the simple psychological reason that a child has no past, he has only a future. That's why he is always ready to learn—in fact, asking too many questions because he wants to know what this life is all about. He harasses his parents by asking questions which the parents themselves don't know how to answer. They don't know the answers either, and they are not courageous enough to say, "We don't know."

An old man has no future, only past. The old man looks backward, not forward. In the future there is only darkness and death, in the past are all his golden memories; he lives in the past. The same is true about countries. A country like India or China has such a long past—they live in the past.

India thinks it has seen its golden age. You will not believe that in India the theory of evolution is not acceptable. India has another theory: the theory of involution. Things are not going, growing, toward better states, evolving—no. Things are falling down—involution. India has the idea that the best age was thousands of years ago; they call it the "age of truth." Then the second stage came, the fall started. They call it simply "the age of three legs." The reason is that the first age they compare to a table with four legs—completely balanced, with no possibility of falling. The second stage has lost one leg, so it is a tripod with three legs, treta—still not too bad, because even with three legs a tripod has a certain balance. The third stage they call dwapar—the age of two legs. Now things are becoming dangerous. A table with two legs—it is not a bicycle, it is bound to fall. The bicycle will also fall unless you go on riding it so that it has no chance to fall. Slow down, and it starts wavering; stop, and it falls. But a table is not a bicycle, so it is bound to fall. The fall is inevitable. The fourth stage has only one leg. They call it "the age of darkness"—kaliyuga. We are living in the age of darkness.

Now, a country which thinks in such terms cannot accept evolution. It has happened—now there is no future. The golden age has come and gone; now there is only darkness and death.

America is just like a child. Three hundred years compared to ninety thousand years—it is just a small child. It has its eyes open, ready to evolve, to grow. It has no past to be bothered about. Gurdjieff is still relevant, and will remain relevant always. People like him never become irrelevant. In spite of the third-rate politicians, America is going to evolve, evolve into the new man, evolve into a new humanity.

I don't want Gurdjieff to become irrelevant. His prophecy has to be fulfilled.

—

Now or Never

Osho,
You have said that the really innovative man comes two hundred years ahead of his time. You also said that time is elastic. Haven't you chosen to come precisely now, before these chaotic times the world is facing, so people will be more receptive to a radical change? And is the ever-faster-growing communication technology not making in this respect the world smaller for your message to spread? Will it really take two hundred years for mankind to open up to your vision?

We are living in a very special time. There are not two hundred years available. If man does not understand my message now, there will be no man after two hundred years to understand. Two hundred years is very long; even twenty years . . . .

Mankind has never been at such a critical moment as it is today. There have been wars—thousands of wars—but they were not going to destroy all life. In the ancient days, wars were almost like football games. The greatest war in India, Mahabharat, happened somewhere around five thousand years ago, and it gives the idea—because that is the only war in India which has been described in such minute detail. Just one family, and two brothers: one brother, who was sick, had five sons; the other brother was blind, but he had one hundred sons. He must have had many women—to manage one hundred sons from one woman is almost impossible. Now the question was, who was going to succeed? The five brothers were very intelligent, courageous, trained in many martial arts. One of them was a great archer; another was a great wrestler; the eldest was a very intelligent man. But the hundred brothers were all what you would call "bad guys"—so everybody wanted the kingdom to go to the five brothers and not to these hundred rascals; even without power they were harassing the people so much. But they were not ready to agree so easily, so the final decision had to be made by war—whoever wins will take over the kingdom.

Now it was a family war, and they invited all their friends, all their relatives—and they were all interrelated. The grandfather, although he loved those five sons, had chosen to be with the one hundred for the simple reason that the five were the sons of a sick man, and a sick man could not rule because of his sickness. So the kingdom had already gone into the hands of the brother with one hundred sons, and to give the kingdom back to the other party would be unfair; although he loved those five and he hated those hundred, still he was fighting with them.

In the evening, as the sun was setting, the war would stop, and people would go into each other's camp. The whole day they were killing each other, and at night they were playing cards, and they were gossiping about the events of the day. That was a totally different kind of war. Man was directly involved, and only soldiers had to fight, not civilians. We have survived thousands of wars of that kind.

But now we are in a very exceptional time. A nuclear war simply means total destruction—a global suicide. Nobody is going to be defeated, nobody is going to be victorious—all are going to be dead. And not only man: birds, animals, trees, all that is living on the earth will be dead. And both the two great powers, America and Russia, go on piling up more and more nuclear weapons. Russia has proved more sensible; seeing the fact that right now we have so many nuclear weapons that every person can be killed seven hundred times— although there is no need to kill any person seven hundred times, once is always enough—the Soviet Union proved far more intelligent than Ronald Reagan. First they tried hard to negotiate that we should stop this piling up of nuclear weapons—it is pointless now, wasting money on it—but Reagan was not willing. So, of their own accord, the Soviet Union for many months did not create any nuclear weapons. They stopped, but America went on piling up more.

The danger is so great that if man can survive, it will be a great miracle. So there is not that much time. For the first time, the future is very short. So in the lifetime of each of you, the decisive moment

is going to come: either man commits suicide or, seeing that this is
an absolute absurdity, man changes his consciousness. It often happens that under pressure people change—and there will never be
again a greater pressure than is present today.

It is most probable that man will go through a transformation. In
that sense my message is exactly at the right time: that nations
should disappear, because it is nations who fight; religions should
disappear, because it is religions who fight. The idea of races—of
superiority and inferiority—should disappear, because that has been
one of the causes of wars. It is a time either to destroy the whole
earth or to destroy all these arbitrary conceptions of nation, race,
religion, and make the whole earth one humanity.

But I do not agree on one point with you. You say, "Have not you
chosen to come precisely now, before these chaotic times the world
is facing?" I have not chosen anything. Perhaps existence has
chosen me to be a vehicle to give you the message—but I have
not chosen. I have disappeared long ago . . . and existence can
speak through you only when you are not. It is hoping against
hope—but I still hope that the danger of global death will be the
shock which awakens humanity. If man survives after this century, it
will be a new man and a new humanity.

One thing is certain: Either man has to die or man has to
change. I cannot think that man will choose to die. The longing for
life is so great . . . just to think that the earth has become dead, no
trees, no humanity, no birds, no animals, no sea animals; it is such a
great crisis. Because in the whole universe . . . it is only an assump-
tion of the scientists that there may be life on fifty thousand planets,
but there is no absolute evidence. It is just a mathematical and logical conclusion, but there is no scientific proof. As far as we know,
only this earth is green, only this earth has flowers, only this earth
has love. Only this earth has produced people like Gautam Buddha,
only this earth has birds which sing, people who dance, people
who love.

This is the only place in the whole universe where people search
and seek for truth. To destroy it—for no particular reason at all—is
such utter stupidity that I don't think that the third world war is going
to happen. And if the third world war does not happen, that will
mean a great change, a tidal change in human consciousness. We
will see a New Man—who is not Christian, not Hindu, who is not a

Jew, who is not a Chinese, who is not an American. If all these trees can exist without being Christians and without being Hindus; if all these birds can exist without any boundaries of nations . . . and when a bird passes the boundary of India and enters Pakistan, he does not need any entry visa, does not even need any passport! Except for mankind, the earth is one. And it is only a question of raising human consciousness.

Nations can disappear, religions can disappear, discriminations can disappear; and with that, much crap will disappear. Politicians will not be of any use; priests will not be of any use; churches and temples and mosques will not be of any use. There are millions of people who don't have homes, and God, who is just a lie, has millions of houses for himself. We have lived in an insane way, and now it is a choice between insanity and sanity.

If insanity wins, there will be no life at all. If sanity wins, life will become for the first time free from all superstitions, all boundaries, all divisions—one humanity, one earth. Freedom of expression, freedom of movement, freedom to choose where you want to live.

It is our earth.

—

Every Woman Should Try to Prevent War

Osho,
Can women do more for peace in the world than men?

Woman certainly can do more for peace in the world, because all the wars are fought by men but suffered by women. Somebody's son dies, somebody's husband dies, somebody's father dies, somebody's brother dies . . . Men fight the war, but the woman is the real sufferer.

You will be surprised to know that whenever an army invades a country, they kill men and they rape women. That is very strange. Even then, there is a difference. They kill the man . . . But they are full of sexuality, repressed sexuality; all soldiers are repressed sexually. Soldiers and monks, these two are the most sexually repressed people in the world.

The woman is the victim: she is raped. And for thousands of years it has been going on.

The woman can do much if she is allowed to have an equal part in all the decisions that are made about life, war, or anything. The woman cannot be for war, and there should be a movement of women against war—it may be man's game but why should woman suffer for it?

And half of humanity consists of women, remember. If half of humanity is against war, it is impossible to bring another war into the world. And woman can fight all efforts against peace in many ways.

Every woman should try to prevent war.

In the old days man has taught woman that when he goes to war she should not cry, she should not weep; on the contrary, she should send her husband with joy, with a prayer in her heart that he becomes a winner. But on the other hand, some other woman is sending her husband with the same prayer to the same God.

If the women decide, "We will not allow our sons to go to war, we will not allow our husbands to go to war, we will not allow our brothers to go to war, we will fight every inch that nobody who is related to us goes to war"—if all the women decide that, then nobody can go to war. It is a simple idea, it just has to be spread.

Right now you have been told to do just the opposite. In the Second World War, women were preparing clothes, sweaters, woolen coats for the soldiers. Not only that, women were even offering their bodies to strange soldiers because they were fighting for the country—and this was thought to be virtuous.

Man is very cunning. He can call anything virtue whenever it is serving his purposes, otherwise it becomes vice—the same thing! For murdering a single man, there is a death penalty. For murdering hundreds of people . . . For the murdering of Hiroshima, Nagasaki, President Truman should have been hanged immediately, so no other politician ever tries any ugly thing like that again. Two hundred thousand people died within five minutes—and for no reason at all, just that President Truman wanted to experiment with the atomic bombs. Using two hundred thousand people as guinea pigs . . . ?

The woman just has to fight it in her family. If every woman fights it in the family and does not allow anybody in the family to go to war, all armies will be dispersed. Force people to come back home, to retire from the army. "We don't want you to get gold medals, we want you to live a human life among human beings."

Woman has never been for war. Her whole life is destroyed by war, she can blossom only in peace. The consciousness of women has to be raised. Millions of men will be in support, millions of my sannyasins will be in support, and millions of other people who have just a little bit of intelligence will be in support.

Just leave the politicians. If they want they can have a wrestling match, a boxing match, do to each other whatever they want to do. "Kill each other, we don't care!" Let their fighting instinct be satisfied. The president of America can have a wrestling match with the president of the Soviet Union, and the whole world can watch on the television and enjoy. It would be such a great entertainment! And who cares who wins or who is defeated? It harms nobody.

The real thing is that the people who create war don't go to war; all the great generals remain behind. Only the poor soldiers are fighting and are being killed. And when the victory is declared, then the victory is of the generals—General Eisenhower becomes victorious, or General MacArthur becomes victorious—and these are the people who have not gone to fight at all. They have been hiding behind, and behind them were their presidents and prime ministers. It is a very strange game. You want to fight, and unnecessarily other people who don't want to fight are being sent to fight and destroy each other.

A world consciousness has to be aroused, so that soldiers—even if they are soldiers—should go to war just to have a chit-chat with the other party and come back . . . and let us see what happens. There is no need to shoot anybody, there is no need to kill anybody. You can play cards, you can do anything for the whole day and come back by the evening.

Man has to become alert that war is so ugly, that it does not suit intelligence—it shows a very retarded mind; it is animalistic. Women can certainly help immensely.

—

A More Human Technology

Osho,
By using modern technology, I feel we are hurting this
vibrating, juicy earth with the dead garbage of plastic,
radioactivity, bad air, and so on. Please would you comment?

It is one of the most complicated questions . . . . It is true: "by using
modern technology we are hurting this vibrating, juicy earth with the
dead garbage of plastic, radioactivity, bad air, and so on." This question has two possible answers.

One is that of Mahatma Gandhi: Go back, to the point where
all modern technology is dropped—which superficially looks right. If
modern technology is creating an ecological crisis on the earth, disturbing the balance of nature, then it is a very simplistic solution to
drop modern technology and go back.

But you have to understand that in Gautam Buddha's time, just
twenty-five centuries ago, India only had twenty million people.
The earth was enough to support them. Today, India alone has
more than nine hundred million people. If you want to go back to
the days of Gautam Buddha, you will have to kill, or allow to die,
such a large part of the population. And when only twenty million
people are saved, and the remainder of the nine hundred million people are lying dead all around you—do you think those
twenty million will be able to live either? And the population goes
on increasing . . . . By the end of the 20th century, the population
of India will have increased by half again. That means it will be
one billion and three-hundred million people—from nearly nine-
hundred to thirteen-hundred million people.

That is why I have disagreed with Mahatma Gandhi on every point. He talks about nonviolence—but this is not nonviolence. Nothing can be more violent a step than this. No war has destroyed so many people as will be destroyed without any war. And it is impossible to live among dead bodies piled up all around you; there will be nobody to take them to the funeral or to take them to the graveyard. So many people dying at such a rate is going to kill the remaining twenty million people too; the rotting bodies will create thousands of diseases, infections.

Mahatma Gandhi used to think that we should stop technology at the point where the spinning wheel was invented. The spinning wheel was invented somewhere around ten thousand years ago, or even earlier. The people were so few, and the earth was so big. The earth was giving so much that those people could not even absorb it all; most of it was going to waste.

So this is one solution, which came to Mahatma Gandhi from Leo Tolstoy—he was also against modern technology. But I cannot support it because it means no railway trains, no hospitals, no surgery, no medicine, no post offices, no telecommunications, no electricity—and all these have become part of your life. You cannot conceive of yourself without electricity! Recently there was just one failure of electricity in America. For three days people were in such a panic, because the elevators were not working, and to go by the stairs in a high-rise building—perhaps one hundred stories, one hundred and twenty stories—just coming down and going up was enough to finish anybody. People became aware for the first time, in those three days in New York, that now there is no possibility of dropping technology.

I have another alternative: It is not the fault of modern technology; the fault is that we have not been very clear what we want from modern technology and what we don't want. The scientist has been discovering almost in a blind way, and whatever he discovers we start using without thinking of the after-effects.

Going back is impossible and idiotic, the only way is forward. We need a better technology—better than the modern technology— so that we can avoid plastic garbage and disturbance of the ecology. The scientist has to be very alert that whatever he is doing should become an intrinsic part of the organic whole; technology should not go against the whole. And it is possible, because technology does not lead you somewhere in particular; it is you who go on discovering things in a blind way. Now it is clear that whatever we have discovered up to now, much of it is a disturbance in the harmony and is finally going to destroy life on the earth—but still, scientists go on piling up nuclear weapons. They don't have the guts to say to the politicians, "It is enough. We are not slaves. We cannot create anything that is going to destroy life."

All the scientists of the world have to come to a consensus. They should create a world academy of sciences which decides what should be discovered and what should not be discovered. If something is discovered that is wrong, it should be undiscovered immediately. We need a superior technology, a more enlightened technology. There I part from Mahatma Gandhi, who goes backward where there is nothing but death. I go forward. Technology is in our hands; we are not in the hands of technology. We can drop all those parts which are dangerous, poisonous, and we can discover substitutes which enhance the ecology, which enhance the life of man, which enhance his outer and inner richness and bring a balance into the world.

But I don't see anybody in the whole world preaching for a more sophisticated, more enlightened technology. Sometimes I wonder: millions of people, thousands of great scientists—are they all blind? Can't they see that what they are doing is cutting their own roots? And if technology can manage to do miracles—which it has managed, on the path of destructiveness—it can also manage miracles on the path of creativeness.

Anything that has been discovered, if it is a disturbance to nature it should be dropped. But I don't see that electricity is a danger to nature; I don't see that railway lines or airplanes are disturbing the ecology; I don't see that innocent telegrams or post offices have to be destroyed. That would be moving to the other extreme. That is how the human mind works—like the pendulum of a clock, from one end to the other end. It never stops in the middle. I want human consciousness to stop exactly in the middle, so that it can see both sides. Certainly, destructiveness cannot be supported; and the energy that goes into creating destructive things must be converted into creativity. But Mahatma Gandhi is not the way. His ideology will prove more dangerous than modern technology has proved. Modern technology may still take hundreds of years to destroy everything. But if we follow Mahatma Gandhi, within a day everything that we have achieved in thousands of years will be destroyed. You could not have cold and hot water in your bathrooms—that depends on modern technology. It is true that it has polluted the air, but that is our fault, not the fault of modern technology. If we had insisted that petrol should be refined to such a point that it did not pollute the air, and that there should be devices in every car to purify the air of whatever damage the petrol was doing, so the balance remained the same.

But in a way, it was natural. You know something only when it has happened. Nobody was aware that going to the moon was creating dangerous holes in the protective shield around the earth. There is a subtle, invisible layer of ozone twenty miles above the earth, all around it. This ozone layer has been protective. It does not allow all the rays of the sun to enter; it allows only the rays which are helpful for life, for trees, for human beings—and the destructive rays are turned back. But nobody was aware of it, so nobody can be blamed for it. When our first rockets went beyond the twenty-mile thick atmosphere, they created holes in the ozone layer; and from those holes, the protective layers disappeared. Now all the rays of the sun can enter through those holes, and this has brought many diseases that were not known before.

But now we can make arrangements, if we want to go to the moon. In the first place, it is lunatic: only people who are in some way mad want to go to the moon. For what?—there is neither water nor greenery nor air to breathe. What is the point of it all? Perhaps military experts may be the only ones who are deeply interested in acquiring the moon—because then the moon can be made a base for throwing nuclear weapons on Russia, if America gets hold of the moon, or if Russia gets hold of the moon, it becomes their territory. But even if you want to go to the moon, you should be careful not to create these holes. And if you are creating them, you should immediately make arrangements that they are covered again, so that destructive rays from the sun cannot reach the earth.

One thing has to be remembered: Man can only go forward; there is no way backward. And there is no point in going backward, either. It is just people's imagination that in the past, when there was no technology, everything was beautiful and good. That is absolutely wrong.

Technology should not be looked at only negatively. In India, just in the nineteenth century, nine children out of ten used to die. Today the situation has reversed: only one child out of ten dies, because of the advancement of medicine. The clothes you are wearing, better houses, lighter and more beautiful houses; there is no need to use heavy material, costly material. Technology is bound to create better food, more proportionate, giving you all the vitamins that are needed and giving you a better taste, too. Technology has a better side also. But if you drop all modern technology, as Gandhi proposed, you will be falling back into the dark ages, and that will be the greatest violence on the earth—preached by the man who thought that his philosophy was nonviolent.

But something has to be done. Up to now, technology has been just groping. Now we can give it a direction; and we can drop all those things which are destructive of ecology, harmony, nature, life. I am all for technology—but a better technology, a more human technology.

—

From Revenge to Compassion

Osho,
What are your suggestions to improve the existing law and
legal systems in the world, so as to make it more effective
and abiding?

I would like to start from a small story. It happened twenty-five cen-
turies ago in China. There was a wise man, Lao Tzu. The emperor of
China appointed him as supreme-most judge of the whole empire.
And Lao Tzu tried to convince the emperor that he would repent:
"Don't do this. I am not going to fit with your legal system because it
is basically wrong. It does not need reformation; it needs revolution."

But the king was stubborn and he insisted, "You become my
supreme judge."

The first case appeared before him in the court: A thief had
stolen from the richest man of the capital, almost half of his treas-
ures. It was a great crime; the legal system prevailing in the country
would give him death. But Lao Tzu also called the rich man to the
court, and said, "Both of these people are criminals, and they both
should be sentenced to jail for six months."

The rich man said, "What kind of justice is this? I have been
robbed! Half of my treasure has been stolen by this man—and you
are punishing me? For what?"

Lao Tzu said, "Because you have accumulated so much money
that it is bound to create thieves in the country. You have been a
criminal first; this man comes in a secondary category."

The rich man rushed to the king and said, "What kind of man
you have chosen to be your supreme judge? He is dangerous! Today

I am going to jail, and tomorrow you will go to jail!"

Of course, immediately Lao Tzu was removed.

You are asking me what improvements, what changes, are needed in the legal system. As I see it, it is basically wrong. It needs nothing less than a revolution; because down the centuries you have been increasing your courts, judges, legal experts, and laws have become more and more complicated every day. And the criminals are increasing tremendously! As the legal system is increasing on one hand, on the other hand crime goes on increasing, and increasing ten times more than your legal system. You have not been able to cope with it. There is something fundamentally wrong.

First, as I see it, the whole legal system is based on social revenge, not on social compassion. The society punishes a person because he was disobedient, because he did not follow the crowd, because he was not part of the mob. He tried to be an individual on his own. He was playing his game according to his own rules. Revenge is not going to help because you are doing the same crime that the criminal has committed. Of course, you have the support of the whole society; so nobody calls your punishment a crime. But any unprejudiced mind can see what you are doing. A man commits rape. A man commits robbery. A man commits murder. Certainly something has to be done, but not punishment. Because if a man commits rape it simply means he is sexually unsatisfied. Your society has not given him a chance to be sexually satisfied.

Muslims are allowed to marry four wives, but in the world there is an equal proportion of men and women. If men are going to marry four wives, then what about those three men who will remain without wives? And if they start committing rape, is it a crime? The Nizam of Hyderabad just a few decades ago is said to have had five hundred wives. And you want to prevent rape? The Maharaja of Patiala was a beautiful man; in Patiala any beautiful woman was in danger of being taken sooner or later. Once the Maharaja looked at her, the next day she would disappear. But he could not manage to take away the daughter of the Viceroy of India, so he raped her. Now, this man seems to be psychologically sick. He has hundreds of wives, concubines, and still he rapes. He does not need punishment, he needs treatment. He should be sent to a psychiatric hospital where his mind can be put right. Something is wrong with his mind. No punishment can change him, because any punishment has nothing to do with psychology.

In fact, once a person goes to jail, the jail becomes his home. He goes there again and again. Jail is a kind of university, because there are the master criminals. When you send somebody to jail for the first time, he is an amateur. But in jail he finds great masters of crime, all the experts. He learns the art, and he learns that it is not the crime that has got him into jail. It is being caught that has brought him into jail. You can go on committing as many crimes as you want, just don't be caught. Because it is not crime that is punished—being caught is punished. This is a strange situation. Those who are caught are in jail. Those who are not caught may be very respectable citizens, powerful people in the society.

I am against all kinds of punishment. The whole idea of punishment is inhuman. Anybody committing a crime simply shows that he needs psychiatric help. Instead of jails, we need psychiatric hospitals where the person can be taken care of respectfully, with dignity. Because once a person's dignity is destroyed, you have reduced him to a permanent criminal. In a psychiatric hospital he should be respected, he should be treated just like any patient.

You will be surprised to know that in the past, many patients were punished for the simple reason that they were not thought to be patients. For example, if somebody was mad, he was punished and sent to a jail. Now we can see the stupidity of it all—a madman, and you are sending him to jail? It is very hard to decide whether you are mad or he is mad. What can the jail do to a madman? He needs a dignified, respectful treatment. And that's what we are doing now.

The same is the situation for other crimes. Crime does not happen out of nowhere; it is something in your mind. Something is wrong, which can be put right. And we have enough development of psychological sciences so that the mind can be changed completely.

One thing is certain: The criminal has a very powerful personality. His personality, his power, if diverted toward creativity may bring great blessings to the society. Right now, these people become a burden on the society. Thousands of people in jail are living on your labor, on your taxes, on your work. And when they come out of jail, they will come with greater expertise, and you will not be able to catch hold of them so easily.

The whole idea of punishment is barbarous. The legal system should change its foundations: every crime should be treated as a mental disease. And then things will be totally different; then the society will be showing compassion, not revenge. And you are helping people to become more human, more integrated. And while they are being treated, you can teach them, you can allow them to learn some skill, some craft, so when they come out of the psychiatric hospital they are not dependent on the society. They can create their living by their own effort, and you have given them so much respect, so much dignity, that it will be impossible for them to commit a crime again.

I am reminded of a mystic who had only one blanket. In the day he used to cover his body with the blanket, in the night he used to cover itself to protect him from the cold. One cold night, a full-moon night, a thief by accident entered his cottage. I say "by accident," because otherwise who goes to a mystic's hut to steal what you can get there? In fact, the mystic was awake, and he had been out for a walk. He entered the hut after the thief. The thief was shocked, embarrassed. The mystic said, "Don't be worried. I have just come in because I have been living in this place for thirty or more years —I have not found anything! Perhaps you can, and we can divide it. I will you join in the search!"

The thief could not believe this man. He said, "I am a thief!"

The mystic said, "Forget all about these adjectives. Who is not a thief? Everybody is stealing something or other. People are stealing knowledge through books, people are stealing every kind of thing; so don't be worried. I am a holy man, and I am joining with you. It is a search! I have been here for thirty years looking for something. There is nothing in this house. Perhaps it is not in my fate; maybe you have a better fate. Something may be found. And I don't ask much, just half the share."

The thief was very puzzled. He had never come across such a man. He said, "Thirty years you have been here and you have not found anything, so there is no possibility. Just let me go. It is so cold, but seeing you I am perspiring. You have made me so nervous, and it is just by accident that I have entered. Forgive me."

The mystic said, "Only on one condition: you will have to take this blanket, because this is the only thing I have got. And you have honored me so much! Because thieves enter kings' palaces—who comes to a poor man's hut? You have honored me—for a moment I feel like a king. So just don't refuse, take this blanket."

The thief could not say anything, but when he saw that the

mystic was naked, he had only the blanket, he felt really sorry for the first time, he felt that he had done something wrong. In his whole life he had never felt that he had done anything wrong. But to face this man was so difficult, to refuse this man was so difficult, so he escaped through the door with the blanket. The mystic shouted, "Stop!"

And the thief stopped and looked back, and he said, "Have I done anything wrong?"

He said, "Yes, at least close the doors. And you have forgotten to give me at least just a thank you. It may help you in the future some time. So say thank you, close the door. And then you can go away wherever you want."

The thief said "Thank you," closed the door, and ran away.

Naked, the saint was sitting near the window, looking at the full moon. And he heard a song. The meaning of the song was, "I am so poor, I could not give him anything more. He must be in desperate need. Otherwise, who comes five miles out of the city to a lonely, isolated hut of a mystic. If it was in my power, I would have given him the full moon. Not less than that. But I am a poor man. I cannot do anything else than give my blanket."

Later on, the thief was caught by the police in another case, was brought to court and asked, "Do you know anybody who can identify you?" He said, "I don't know anybody except a mystic who lives outside the city. Perhaps he can recognize me."

The saint was called to the court. He recognized the thief, and he said to the magistrate, "Don't punish this poor man. I gave him my blanket, he has not stolen it. And he is a very graceful gentleman. Not only has he not stolen my blanket, he said, 'Thank you, sir.' And when I said to him, 'Close the doors,' he was so obedient, he closed the doors. He is a very humble man. Forgive him."

The mystic was very much respected in the surroundings. The magistrate himself was a follower of the mystic. When he said, "Forgive him," the magistrate forgave him. As the mystic was leaving the court, he found the thief following him. He said, "Why are you following me?"

He said, "Now I am going to be with you forever. I have never come across a man who has ever respected me as a human being. You have given me dignity. Others have treated me like a dog, a thief. And the more they have mistreated me, the more I have done the

same things, out of revenge. You are the only man who has not bothered about my actions, but you have looked directly into my eyes and
into my being. I am not going to leave you." The thief became a saint
in his own way. He became the successor of the old saint.

The whole legal system needs to drop revengefulness. It has to
become compassionate; it has to treat human beings with respect.

Actions don't count. What counts is the whole personality, which
is a vast thing. An action is a small thing. Don't make it too big.
And we are making it too big. Somebody does something wrong
– and remember, it is human to err; everybody commits mistakes.
But the mistakes should not be taken as equivalent to his life. It is
only a small fragment in a long series. Don't give it too much importance. Don't make it the focus. Don't throw that man into jail, undig-
nified, unhonored, all his humanity taken away. Don't behave with
that man as if he is an animal.

Society needs to be more compassionate. The law needs to be
more compassionate. Remember, man is not for the law; the law is for
man. And if the law is not helping man, then it has to be changed.

It has not helped—there is no doubt about it. And I am not saying
withdraw all laws and dissolve all courts. I am saying that your courts
and your laws and your legal experts should make the whole phenomenon based on compassion, not on revenge. Compassion is the
essence of all religions. And if we cannot create our legal system based
on the essential, fundamental religious experience of the ages, then
future will condemn us; then future will think about us as barbarous,
then future is not going to accept us as civilized, cultured people.

We are still living in a barbarous age. Perhaps we have better
clothes, better houses, polite, nice manners, beautiful masks to hide
our faces. But deep down, there is an animal who hankers for
revenge. It is strange to see that still there are countries where the
death sentence is legal. If a man has murdered someone, and you
think it is a crime ...

It certainly is a crime. Nobody has the right to destroy somebody else's life. But what are you doing? You destroy that man's
life? And I don't see the logic. If this man's murder, crucifixion, was
going to revive the other man, then there might be some logic in it.
But instead of one man dead, now there will be two men dead, and
you think that the law is satisfied, the society is satisfied. But this
satisfaction is ugly.

So I will not go into the details of law, because that is not my function. My function is to change the foundation. Then the details will change automatically. Up to now, revenge has been the foundation. Let compassion be the foundation in the future.

It is a very strange experience: I have been visiting jails, teaching prisoners meditation, and I was surprised that they are more innocent than your judges, than your lawyers, than your lawmakers. They are more innocent people. I have been in jail in America for twelve days, and that has given me a great experience, from the inside. I had been to jails before, but I was an outsider. This time I was an insider, an inmate, and I was surprised to know, utterly surprised, that the people you have condemned as criminals, condemned for their whole life to live in darkness, in dismal cells—which is worse than death—are far more innocent, loving, understanding.

In twelve days I was in six jails, because the authorities were afraid to keep me in one jail. It was surrounded by news media, by sannyasins, by people who love me, and the jail authorities were afraid that something might go wrong. So they went on changing me from one jail to another. It was good for me, because I came to know hundreds of criminals, and not a single person in those six jails—and each jail had five hundred, six hundred, seven hundred people—not a single criminal was against me. They were all in favor of me, because they were seeing my statements on the television. And when I passed through the cells, every criminal was showing me the sign of victory, and they were shouting in different languages, "Don't be worried, final victory is yours!"

I would ask the jail authorities for small things—a toothbrush, toothpaste, a soap, a towel, a comb—and it would take twelve hours for the toothbrush to appear, but there was no toothpaste! And if the toothpaste appeared, then there was no toothbrush. If the soap appeared, then there was no towel. I could not take a shower. But I was amazed that these criminals would go on throwing things into my cell. And they would say, "This is absolutely new, we have not used it. This toothbrush, you can see it is still sealed; we have been keeping it, we had never known that this would be our blessing to give it to you."

I would ask for milk, and the answer was no. And some criminal would bring his own milk, and one of them said, "These people are simply harassing you. Every inmate is getting milk, and to you they

say there is no milk, no fruit"—knowing perfectly well that I am vegetarian and I would not be eating anything else than fruit and
vegetables, milk. You will be surprised that in those twelve days
whatever I was eating was given to me by the criminals, not by the
jail authorities. Out of their own—because they used to get one
apple every day, and if I was in a cell where there were six people,
they would all bring me their apples. I had six apples. I would say,
"I cannot eat six apples. And as you are all Christians, you know
well that Adam and Eve just ate one apple, and humanity is still
suffering, and you are giving me six! Do you want me to get out of
jail or not?"

I came to see that we are not doing justice to these people. Their
small act—maybe in a fit of anger they did something—and it
has become their whole life. You have not given them a chance
to change. You have finished them, you have put a full stop. Just a
small fit of anger, and a man may have done something. What he
needs is to be taught how anger can be dispersed, how one can get
above anger—but this you are not doing. By forcing him into jail,
you are making the man angrier. You are creating more criminals.

Your whole legal system is a criminal system.

Public Servants, Missionaries, and Their Kind

Osho,
You teach your people to take care of themselves before they
try to take care of others. This seems to go against many of the
religions in the world that teach service to humanity, and it
must appear a very selfish attitude to them. Can you speak on
this?

It not only goes against many religions, it goes against all the religions in the world. They all teach service to others, unselfishness.
But to me, selfishness is a natural phenomenon. Unselfishness is
imposed. Selfishness is part of your nature. Unless you come to a
point where your self dissolves into the universal, you cannot be
truly unselfish. You can pretend, but you will only be a hypocrite,
and I don't want my people to be hypocrites. So it is a little complicated, but it can be understood.

First, selfishness is part of your nature. You have to accept it.
And if it is part of your nature it must be serving something very
essential, otherwise it would not have been there at all. It is because
of selfishness that you have survived, that you have taken care of
yourself; otherwise humanity would have disappeared long ago. Just
think of a child who is unselfish, born unselfish. He will not be able
to survive, he will die—because even to breathe is selfish, to eat is
selfish, when there are millions of people who are hungry and you
are eating, when there are millions of people who are unhealthy,
sick, dying, and you are healthy.

If a child is born without selfishness as an intrinsic part of his
nature, he is not going to survive. If a snake comes close to him,

what is the need to avoid the snake? Let him bite. It is your selfishness that protects you; otherwise, you are coming in the way of the snake. If a lion jumps upon you and kills you, be killed. That is unselfishness. The lion is hungry, you are providing food—who are you to interfere? You should not protect yourself, you should not fight. You should simply offer yourself on a plate to the lion. That will be unselfishness. All these religions have been teaching things which are unnatural. This is only one of the things.

I teach you nature. I teach you to be natural, absolutely natural, unashamedly natural. Yes, I teach you selfishness. Nobody has said it before me. They had not the guts to say it. And they were all selfish; this is the amazing part of the whole story. Why is a Jaina monk torturing himself? There is a motivation. He wants to attain moksha and all the pleasures therein. He is not sacrificing anything, he is simply bargaining. He is a businessman, and his scriptures say, "You will get a thousandfold." And this life is really very small—seventy years is not much. If you sacrifice seventy years' pleasures for an eternity of pleasures it is a good bargain. I don't think it is unselfish.

And why have these religions been teaching you to serve humanity? What is the motive? What is the goal? What are you going to gain out of it? You may never have asked the question. This is not service.

I have loved a very ancient Chinese story: A man falls into a well. It was at a big gathering, a festival time, and there was so much noise, and people were enjoying, dancing, singing, and all kinds of things were going on, so nobody heard him fall. And at that time in China wells were not protected by a wall surrounding them, at least four or five feet high so nobody falls in. They were without any protection, just open. You could fall in the darkness without being aware that there is a well.

The man starts shouting, "Save me!"

A Buddhist monk passes by. Of course a Buddhist monk is not interested in the festival, is not supposed to be interested—I don't know what he was doing there. Even to be there means some unconscious urge to see what is going on, how people are enjoying: "All these people will go to hell, and I am the only one here who is going to heaven." He passes by the well, and he hears this man. He looks down. The man says, "Good that you have heard me. Everybody is so busy and there is so much noise that I was afraid I was going to die."

The Buddhist monk says, "You are still going to die, because this is from your past life's evil act: now you are getting the punishment. Get it and be finished! It is good. In the new life you will come out clean, and there will be no need to fall again into a well."

The man says, "I don't want any wisdom and any philosophy at this moment." But the monk had moved on.

A Taoist, old man, stops. He is thirsty, looks in. The man is still crying for help. The Taoist says, "This is not manly. One should accept everything as it comes—that's what the great Lao Tzu has said. So accept it! Enjoy! You are crying like a woman. Be a man!"

The man says, "I am ready to be called a woman, but first please save me! I am not manly. And you can say anything that you want to say afterward—first pull me out."

But the Taoist says, "We never interfere in anybody's business. We believe in the individual and his freedom. It is your freedom to fall in the well, it is your freedom to die in the well. All that I can do is just suggest to you that to die crying, weeping, is foolish. You can die like a wise man—accept it, enjoy it, sing a song, and go. Anyway, everybody is going to die, so what is the point of saving you? I am going to die, everybody is going to die—perhaps tomorrow, perhaps the day after tomorrow—so what is the point of bothering to save you?" And he moves on.

A Confucian comes, and the man sees some hope, because Confucians are more worldly, more earthbound. He says, "It is my good fortune that you have come, a Confucian scholar. I know you, I have heard your name. Now do something for me, because Confucius says, 'Help others.'" After seeing the Buddhist and the Taoist, the man thinks, "It is better to talk philosophy if these people are to be convinced to save me." He says, "Confucius says, 'Help others.'"

The Confucian monk says, "You are right. And I will help. I am going from one city to another, and I will try and protest and force the government to make a protective wall around every well in the country. Don't be afraid."

The man says, "But by the time those protective walls are made and your revolution succeeds, I will be gone!"

The Confucian says, "You don't matter, I don't matter, individuals don't matter—society matters. You have raised a very significant question by falling in the well. Now we are going to fight for it. Be calm and quiet. We will see that every well has a protective wall around it so nobody falls into it. Just by saving you, what is saved? The whole country has millions of wells, and millions of people can fall into them. So don't be too selfish about yourself, rise above this selfish attitude. I am going to serve humanity—you have served by falling into the well, I am going to serve by forcing the government to make protective walls." And he walks on. But he makes a significant point: "You are very selfish. You just want to be saved and waste my time, which I can use for the whole of humanity." Do you know if anything like "humanity" exists anywhere, if anything like a "society" exists anywhere? These are just words. Only individuals exist.

The fourth man is a Christian minister, a missionary, who is carrying a bag with him. He immediately opens the bag, takes out a rope, throws the rope. Even before the man says anything, he throws the rope into the well. The man is surprised. He says, "Your religion seems to be the truest religion."

He says, "Of course. We are prepared for every emergency. Knowing that people can fall into wells, I am carrying this rope to save them, because only by saving them can I save myself. But remember—I have heard what the Confucian was saying—don't make protective walls around the wells; otherwise how will we serve humanity? How will we pull out people from wells who fall in? They have to fall first, only then can we pull them out. We exist to serve, but the opportunity must be there. Without the opportunity, how can you serve?"

All these religions talking about service are certainly interested that humanity remains poor, that people remain in need of service, that there are orphans, there are widows, old people nobody takes care of, beggars. These people are needed, absolutely needed. Otherwise, what will happen to these great servants of the people? What will happen to all these religions and their teachings? And how will people enter the Kingdom of God? These people have to be used as a ladder.

Do you call it unselfishness? Is this missionary unselfish? He is not saving this man for this man's sake; he is saving this man for his own sake. Deep down it is still selfishness, but now it is covered with beautiful words: "unselfishness, service."

But why is there any need for service? Why should there be any need? Can't we destroy these opportunities for service? We can, but the religions will be very angry. Their whole ground will be lost—this is their whole business—if there is nobody poor, nobody hungry, nobody suffering, nobody sick. And science can make it possible. It is absolutely in our hands today. It would have been long ago, if these religions had not stopped every person who was going to contribute to knowledge, which can destroy all the opportunities for service. But these religions have been against all scientific progress, and they will talk of service. They need these people. Their need is not unselfish; it is utterly selfish. It is motivated. There is a goal to be achieved.

Hence I say to my sannyasins, service is a dirty, four letter word. Never use it. Yes, you can share, but never humiliate anybody by serving him. It is humiliation. When you serve somebody and you feel great, you have reduced the other into a worm, subhuman. And you are so superior that you have sacrificed your own interests and you are serving the poor. You are simply humiliating them.

If you have something, something that gives you joy, peace, ecstasy, share it. And remember that when you share, there is no motive. I am not saying that by sharing it you will reach heaven. I am not giving you any goal. I am saying to you, just by sharing it you will be tremendously fulfilled. In the very sharing is the fulfilment, there is no goal beyond it. It is not end-oriented, it is an end unto itself, and you will feel obliged to the person who was ready to share with you. You will not feel that he is obliged to you, because you have not served.

Only these people who believe in sharing instead of service can destroy all those opportunities, those ugly opportunities which surround the whole earth. And all the religions have been exploiting those opportunities. But they give good names...they have become very proficient, in thousands of years, in giving good names to ugly things. And when you start giving a beautiful name to an ugly thing, there is a possibility you yourself may forget that it was just a cover. Inside, the reality is just the same.

All these religions have given good names, beautiful names, to ugly realities. Why serve the poor when poverty can be destroyed? No religion says, "Destroy poverty." They are in deep conspiracy with the vested interests. They don't say destroy poverty, they don't suggest any measures for how poverty can be destroyed, stopped. But serve the poor, serve the widows. They don't say, "Why force the woman to remain a widow?" So simple a phenomenon . . . In India the man is allowed to get married as many times as he wants.

In fact the moment the wife dies, her body is being burned on the funeral pyre and people are beginning to talk about marriage, where to arrange this man's next marriage. So ugly, so inhuman—the body of the wife is not yet burned completely...but sitting around there, what else to do? They have to talk about something, and this is the hottest topic. Now this man needs a woman, and they are suggesting where it will be good to marry, which woman will be suitable for him—and not a widow. Nobody is ready to get married to a widow. She is a used woman. Woman is a thing, used by somebody else—how can you use it? Man is not used; he always remains fresh, pure. He can get remarried.

In India for thousands of years the woman has suffered so much because of this idea that she has to remain a widow. Millions of widows...they cannot wear any other color than white. They have to shave their heads, they cannot wear any ornaments. In every possible way it has been made clear to them that they have to live almost a dead life. They cannot move in the society as other women do—particularly in festivals, they are not supposed to. At marriages they are not supposed to be present because their very presence, their very shadow, is a calamity. And the widow is told that she has eaten her husband—it is because of her fate that the husband died. If he had not married her he would be alive; she is responsible for his death. The whole life she carries this burden, and now she has to remain in every way ugly.

"Serve the widows." In India there are institutions especially for widows, because in homes they are not even equal to the servants. They do all kinds of work, the whole day they work. But they don't get any respect: no salary, no respect, and continuous condemnation that because of them somebody's son has died, somebody's brother has died. Everybody is against the woman, and she has to remain hidden like a shadow. She is not allowed to be there when guests are there. She lives like a ghost. So institutions are opened by religions; this is service for the widows. But why have widows in the first place? It is such a simple logic: make it a law that any man who wants to marry a second time has to marry a widow, not a virgin— simple. And the whole problem disappears. Rather than making the problems disappear, you help them to continue.

Now the same thing is happening in the West, in other ways, in other directions. Medical science has evolved so much that the scientists say that there is no intrinsic necessity for the human body to die for at least three hundred years. And this is a conservative estimate, three hundred years. They say for three hundred years there is no intrinsic necessity for the human body to die. For three hundred years everybody can live fully—young. And if one can live three hundred years, can you think what the implications of it will be? Just think—Albert Einstein living three hundred years. What blessings would he not have showered on humanity! Such a mature mind! At the age of twenty-six he was able to present the theory of relativity, which transformed the whole of science and its shape. Just think, if he was able to live for three hundred years, all that seems impossible would have been possible through him. And I am taking just one example.

If Bertrand Russell can give so much in one hundred years, then in three hundred years . . . It is not possible for a man like Bertrand Russell to sit and not do anything. Even when he was a hundred years old he was far younger than your so-called young people—in his vision, in his approach, in his reasoning, in his clarity about everything. And if this man had been able to live three hundred years, I can say with absolute certainty that he would have changed many things that he had said when he was fifty, forty, thirty. He may have turned inward, he may have become a meditator. He may have proved to be one of the greatest religious men on the earth. He had every capacity, and he had all the courage that is needed to use that capacity. But the time was short.

A hundred years for a man like Bertrand Russell is very short. He had such a multidimensional interest: in education he wanted to create a revolution; in philosophy he brought new concepts into existence; in mathematics...which was not his subject, but he was so interested in logic that he was compelled to go into mathematics, because they function on the same lines. Mathematics is logic applied. Russell joined hands with one of the great mathematicians and philosophers of America, Whitehead, and together they wrote a book, *Principia Mathematica*. It is so far ahead of its time—even today there are only perhaps a dozen or two dozen people who can understand it, what it is. If he had lived three hundred years he would have given you a totally new mathematics, perhaps a higher mathematics about which Gurdjieff, Ouspensky—mystics like these people—were interested, a higher mathematics which does not deal with ordinary material experiments but which deals with ultimate problems. And your mathematics that you learn in the universities cannot deal with the ultimate problems. Ultimate problems are beyond it. A totally new mathematics is needed, because when you come closer to the ultimate you find all your categories, logic, mathematics, falling apart. Existence behaves differently—so differently that sometimes two plus two can be three, sometimes two plus two can be five. One thing is certain: at the ultimate, two plus two are never four.

I can give you a simple example. Why can two plus two never be four at the ultimate core of existence? It is because no two things are exactly similar. Two chairs are not exactly the same. Two other chairs are not exactly the same. You put all of them together, and you call it four chairs—and they are not the same, each chair is different. To be absolutely right, you cannot use four. The electrons, the protons, the neutrons—the world deep at the ultimate core behaves in a totally different way. If you go out of a room, we know that you can only go out of the room if you pass through a certain passage, maybe ten steps; then you reach outside. But you will be there, in each of the ten, each time you take a step. But at the ultimate level, the electron jumps without being in between. It is at point a, then it is found at point b, which is far away from a, but it is not found between the two at all. From a it disappears and appears at b, and between the two there is no passage. Now, how can your ordinary mathematics, measurements, geometry, function? Something totally different is needed.

And as man's life has grown longer, we have been able to discover science. You may not have thought about it. Science has come into existence only in the last three hundred years—why? Why not before? We have not been able to find a single skeleton of a human being who lived three thousand years ago—to say nothing about further back—which is older than forty years. The man must have died at the age of forty. Forty must have been the age limit sometime, because we have not found a single skeleton which proves that the man died at fifty, sixty, seventy; forty is the oldest.

So there is nothing strange when the Vedas say—and Hindus think it is something of tremendous glory to them—that people never got old. Hindus think that in the times of the Vedas, science must have been so advanced that nobody was ever old. That is not the truth. The truth is everybody was dying at forty, so how could one get old? When man started living longer, and seventy became the average age—and in Western countries, in some countries eighty, in some countries ninety became the average age—then science developed. Otherwise, in forty years what can a person do? He is just trying somehow to survive—himself, his wife, a line of children—and then comes death. Science or philosophy or religion or anything higher needs more time, more luxury, more comfort. Now man can live three hundred years. And if man can live three hundred years, why not six hundred? Why not one thousand? Once man comes to live three hundred years it is absolutely certain we will find there are ways to make him live longer. Then he becomes accumulated wisdom. Then he can work out complicated problems.

Solve the problems! There is no need to teach people service. What are the problems? The population explosion is the problem. All the religions are teaching, "Serve the poor," but not a single religion is ready to say, "Accept birth control so that the population is reduced."

I am for absolute birth control. Only a few people should be allowed to give birth to children, and that too should be done by artificial insemination—because what is the need? It is possible that you fall in love with a girl, that the girl falls in love with you, but you may not be the right persons to become parents, to give birth to a child. You may not be, because love takes no account of your inner chemistry.

You don't go to the chemist to find out, "I am falling in love with this girl; do our inner chemistries meet?" If you go at all, you go to the idiot astrologer, the palmist—the blind leading the blind. It is a biochemical question, nothing to do with palmistry, nothing to do with astrology. But man's ego feels as if stars are interested in him. Just think of the stupidity of the whole idea that millions of stars are concerned with you, and are affecting you, and their combinations are affecting you. It just makes me feel sad about man. What kind of humanity has grown up on the earth?

But all these religions are against birth control, and without birth control there is no way now. I am in support of absolute birth control, remember, not just birth control; because with birth control, people—if not religions, then governments—are compelled to accept that they should have only two children or three children. No, that won't do. Even two, three children won't do. Absolute birth control: nobody should be allowed to give birth to children; anybody

who is interested in children can go, contribute his semen to the scientific lab, and the lab should decide who is going to be the woman
for your child's mother.

It need not be your wife, there is no relationship in it. You love
your wife, your wife loves you, but that does not mean burden the
earth with a crippled, blind child. You don't have that power, you
don't have that permission from existence. Why are you taking such
an irresponsible burden on yourself and on the whole of humanity?
You give birth to a child who is crippled, or blind, or mad, or insane,
and he will give birth to other children. That's how the idiots are
always in the majority in the world. They are bound to be, because
the right combination can happen only through a scientific lab. You
cannot...you don't know what you are carrying in your genes;
you don't know what your potential is, what kind of child you are
going to give birth to. You love the woman—there is no harm in that;
love should be absolutely available to you, that is your birthright.
You love the woman; but every woman need not be a mother, every
man need not be a father. Soon there will be no need for the mother,
either. The child can grow in the scientific lab itself.

You want a child, and if you really love children you would
like the best child possible. So who contributes the semen and who
contributes the mother's womb should not be your concern. Your
concern should be that you get the best child possible. So I suggest
artificial insemination and test-tube babies.

And I also suggest euthanasia. Just as we are putting a barrier
on birth, birth control, let me give you another term, death control.
After a certain age—for example, if you accept seventy as the
average, or eighty or ninety as the average—a man should be free to
ask the medical board, "I want to be freed from my body." He
has every right, if he does not want to live anymore, because he has
lived enough; he has done everything that he wanted to do. And
now he wants not to die of cancer or tuberculosis; he simply wants
a relaxed death. Every hospital should have a special place for
people, with a special staff, where people can come, get relaxed and
be helped to die beautifully, without any disease, supported by the
medical profession. Unless the medical board feels that the person is
valuable—for example, somebody like Einstein or Bertrand Russell
—unless the medical board feels that the person is of immense
importance, then he can be asked to live a little longer. Only a

few people should be asked to be here a little longer because they can be so much help to humanity, so much help to others. But if even those people don't want to live, that is their birthright. You can pray, ask, request. If they accept it, good. But if they say, "No, we are not interested anymore," then certainly they have every right to die.

Why should a person be forced to live when he does not want to live? And you make it a crime, you make the man unnecessarily worried: he does not want to live but he has to live because suicide is a crime. He has to take poison, or he has to jump into the ocean or from a hill. This is not a good situation. And strange: if he dies, good; if he is caught then he will be sentenced to death. Great society! Great minds creating laws! He will be sentenced to death because he was trying to commit suicide.

All these problems can be solved. Hence there is no need for public servants, missionaries, and their kind. We need more intelligence brought to the problem and how to solve it.

So I teach selfishness. I want you to be, first, your own flowering. Yes, it will appear as selfishness; I have no objection to that appearance of selfishness. It is okay with me. But is the rose selfish when it blossoms? Is the lotus selfish when it blossoms? Is the sun selfish when it shines? So why should you be worried about selfishness?

You are born: birth is only an opportunity, just a beginning, not the end. You have to flower. Don't waste it in any kind of stupid service. Your first and foremost responsibility is to blossom, to become fully conscious, aware, alert; and in that consciousness you will be able to see what you can share, how you can solve problems. Ninety-nine percent of the world's problems can be solved. Perhaps one percent of problems may not be solved. Then you can share with those people whatever you can share—but first you have to have something to share.

All these religions up to now have not helped humanity in solving a single problem. Just look at what I am saying: have they solved a single problem? And they have been doing this service business for millions of years. The poor are still poor, and go on growing poorer. The sick are there, old age is there, all kinds of diseases are there, all kinds of crimes are there—and they go on increasing. Every year there are more crimes in the world than the last year. Strange... prisons go on increasing, courts go on increasing—and they think they are there to stop crime, and with them the crime goes on increasing. Something is basically wrong somewhere. What they are doing is unrelated to the problem. The person who is committing a crime is not a criminal, he is a sick person. He need not be thrown into jail and tortured, he has to be put into a psychiatric hospital and served there, medically, respectfully. It is not his fault.

You must know there was a time when mad people were thought to be criminals and they were thrown into prison, and there they were beaten. It was only a few hundred years ago that it occurred to anyone that these people are not criminals, they are suffering from a certain disease. By beating them you cannot beat the disease out. You are simply being idiotic. They need treatment, and you are mistreating them. And the same is true about all criminals, because I don't see that any criminal is a born criminal. The way he is brought up, the society in which he is brought up, makes him a criminal. And once his mind starts becoming criminal, then you have to change the whole way of his mind. It is no use chaining him, throwing him into jail, starving him, beating him—it does nothing. It is simply reinforcing in him that when he comes out he will be a confirmed criminal, a graduated criminal.

You have to change the track of his mind which moves into criminality. And that can be done. Biochemistry can be of much help, medicine can be of much help, psychiatry can be of much help. Now we have every resource to make that man a dignified human being.

Service is not needed, what is needed is a sharing of your consciousness—your knowledge, your being, your respect—but first you must have it.

To me the greatest problem with humanity is that they don't know anything of meditation. To me, that is the greatest problem. Neither the population, nor the atom bomb, nor hunger...no, these are not basic problems; they can be easily solved by science. The only, basic problem that science will not be able to solve is that people don't know how to meditate.

To my people I say: first be selfish, utterly selfish—blossom. Come to flowering and fragrance, and then spread it. Then share it with those unfortunate people who had the same potential as you, but life has not given them the chance to go inward, to have a taste of their own godliness.

I am against all the religions because to me, what they have done is absolutely useless. But they "do" with beautiful words, and they hide things in beautiful words. You can use beautiful words, beautiful phrases to hide some ugly truth. I don't want to do that kind of job at all.

I teach you to be natural, and I teach you to accept your naturalness. I know one thing for certain, that when you have blossomed, you will be sharing. There is no way to avoid it. When the flower opens up there is no way for it to prevent its fragrance and keep it imprisoned. The fragrance escapes. It reaches in all directions. So first, be fulfilled, be content. First, be. Then out of your being there will be a fragrance reaching to many. And it will not be a service, it will be a sheer, joyous sharing. And there is nothing more joyful than sharing your joy.

—

Whatever the Consequence, Be True

Osho,
For my whole life, friendliness has been a shield for me to
protect myself from others. Now layers of this shield are
dropping away, more and more, and I feel a space in which I
am enough unto myself. Out of this space, a more open and
less fearful connection happens. And yet, I often watch myself
not being totally authentic and real. Why is this so difficult?

One of the problems that every human being has to face is the world
in which he is born. His being and the intentions of the world don't
go together. The world wants him to serve, to be a slave, to be used
by those who are in power. And naturally he resents it. He wants to
be himself. The world does not allow anybody to be what he is by
nature supposed to be.

The world tries to mold every person into a commodity: useful,
efficient, obedient—never rebellious, never asserting itself, never
declaring its own individuality, but always being subservient, almost
like a robot. The world does not want you to be human beings. It wants
you to be efficient machines. The more efficient you are, the more
respectable, the more honored. And this is what creates the problem.
No individual is born here to be a machine. It is a humiliation, a degra-
dation; it is taking away his pride and dignity, destroying him as a spiritual being and reducing him into a mechanical entity.

Hence every child, from the very beginning, as he becomes
aware of the intentions of the society, of the parents, of the family, of
the educational system, of the nation, of the religion—as he becomes
aware, he starts closing himself. He starts becoming defensive just

out of fear, because he has to encounter a tremendous force. And he is so small and so fragile, so vulnerable, so helpless, so dependent on the same people against whom he has to protect himself.

And the problem becomes more complicated because the people he has to protect himself against are the people who think that they love him. And perhaps they are not lying. Their intentions are good, but their consciousness is missing; they are fast asleep. They don't know that they are being puppets in the hands of a blind force called the society, the establishment—all the vested interests are together.

The child faces a dilemma. He has to fight against those whom he loves, and he thinks they love him too. But it is strange that the people who love him don't love him as he is. They say to him, "We will love you, we do love you, but only if you follow the way we are following, if you follow the religion we are following, if you become obedient the way we are obedient." If you become part of this vast mechanism, in which you are going to live your whole life . . . fighting against it is simply meaningless, you will be crushed. It is wiser just to surrender and just to learn to say yes, whether you want to or not. Repress your no. In all conditions, in all situations, you are expected to be a yea-sayer. The no is prohibited. The no is the original sin. Disobedience is the original sin—and then the society takes revenge with a great vengeance.

This creates great fear in the child. His whole being wants to assert its potential. He wants to be himself because other than that he cannot see any meaning in life. Other than that, he will never be happy, joyous, fulfilled, contented. He will never feel at ease, he will always be in a split. A part, the most intrinsic part of his being, will always feel hungry, thirsty, unfulfilled, incomplete.

But the forces are too big and to fight against them is too risky. Naturally every child, slowly, slowly starts learning to defend himself, to protect himself. He closes all the doors of his being. He does not expose himself to anybody, he simply starts pretending. He starts being an actor. He acts according to the orders given to him. Doubts arise in him, he represses them. His nature wants to assert itself, he represses it. His intelligence wants to say, "This is not right, what are you doing?"—he drops being intelligent. It is safer to be retarded, it is safer to be unintelligent. Anything that brings you in conflict with the vested interests is dangerous. And to open yourself, even to people who are very close, is risky.

Machiavelli, one of the most intelligent persons who has ever walked on the earth—but who misused his intelligence, misused his genius—says in his masterpiece *The Prince*, "Don't say anything, even to your friend, unless you are willing to say it to your enemy; because nobody knows . . . tomorrow the friend can turn into your enemy." Never say anything against the enemy that you are not ready to say against the friend; because who knows? Tomorrow the enemy may become your friend; then you will feel embarrassed. So be alert and cautious, take every step thinking of all the pros and cons.

But this kind of life cannot be a joyous life; it will be cunning, it will be clever. It may achieve comfortable living, luxurious living, it may become successful in the world, but it will not achieve any at-ease-ness. It will not find any peace with existence, with oneself. Deep down there will remain the child—crushed, crippled, doing everything against his will.

Machiavelli was teaching people to be cunning. From all the royal families of Europe, princes were sent to learn diplomacy—in other words, hypocrisy, in other words politics, the ability to commit crimes without being caught. And he was teaching these people; only princes were his disciples. He was earning enough, and when these princes became kings in their own right, he thought that it was time he should become a prime minister—because almost all the kings of Europe were his disciples, and none could refuse. But he was refused by everybody, without exception. They all said, "We love you, we respect you, but we cannot take the risk of making you the prime minister because you are too clever. Our whole kingdom will be at risk. We cannot take that risk. It is according to your teachings. You have told us, 'Never allow more intelligent people than you in your court because they will be, sooner or later, a danger to your position, to your power. They will become your competitors. Always keep a distance. Remain surrounded by mediocres.'" Hence, every politician who is in power remains surrounded by mediocres. He finds people who are at such a distance that they cannot dream of taking away his power or his position. People who are too close are dangerous.

But such is the worldly teaching. That's why everybody has become closed. Nobody opens one's petals fearlessly like a flower, dancing in the wind, and in the rain, and in the sun . . . so fragile but without any fear. We are all living with closed petals, afraid that if we open up we will become vulnerable. So everybody is using shields of all kinds—even a thing like friendliness, you say, you have been using as a shield. It will look contradictory, because friendliness means openness to each other, sharing each other's secrets, sharing each other's hearts.

But it is not only the case with you. Everybody is living in such contradictions. People are using friendliness as a shield, love as a shield, prayer as a shield. When they want to cry they cannot cry, they smile, because a smile functions as a shield. When they don't feel like crying they cry, because tears can function in certain situations as a shield.

I used to live with one of my uncles. His sister was old, and she had come from a faraway village to be treated in the city. So she was staying with us. Then she died.

I used to sit outside the bungalow in the garden, either working in the garden or reading—but most of the time I was in the garden. My uncle would go to his shop, and only my aunt remained in the house. She told me, "You have to ring the bell if you see somebody is coming to show mourning for your uncle's sister's death, because I don't feel like crying or weeping. I had no feeling for that woman. In fact, she was an unnecessary burden, she was of no use to anybody. Everybody feels relieved, but nobody can say that. We have to cry and weep when relatives come to show mourning." This continues in India for almost a month. So she said, "I don't want to be caught in the middle of something—somebody suddenly comes and I am smiling or laughing or talking with somebody, and I am supposed to be weeping."

So I used to ring the bell to let her know that somebody has come—there was an electric bell there. I used to ring the bell and she would immediately change her whole demeanor completely. She would pull down her ghunghat so that nobody could see her face, because the face might be still smiling and tears were coming; and those were false tears. Seeing the use of her ghunghat, I saw that the sari in India is certainly more useful than anything else. You can hide your face completely behind it. Otherwise it is very difficult to show pain, misery, anguish, anxiety, when you are not feeling any of those things; rather you are feeling relieved, your prayer has been heard. Everybody wanted this woman to die, because everybody was tired and she was going on and on.

One day I did not ring the bell, and one of the relatives entered the house. My aunt was watching television and laughing and enjoying. She was alone in the room, and this man entered from the back. He was very shocked. He said, "I had never thought that I would have to see this." She pulled her ghunghat and immediately started crying—it was so absurd, it made no sense—but she was very angry with me. When the man was gone, she came out and started shouting at me.

I said, "What could I do if the electricity failed, or something went wrong?" I had taken out the wires, because otherwise she would have killed me! She would have been ferocious. So I said, "I rang the bell, but what could I do? How could I know that the wires were not joined with the bell?" She looked at the wires. She said, "But who could have done it? You and I are the only two persons here."

I said, "I can say only one thing: I have not done it. I cannot say anything about you. And who knows? Your husband may have done it for some reason before going to the shop. Nobody knows . . . just wait, we will try to find out; but unless we have found out who has done it, your being angry at me is not right. And remember that I have been giving you the signal up to now. From now onward, it is finished. I am not going to ring the bell. You stay prepared."

She cooled down, seeing the situation. She said, "Forget it. What happened, happened. But don't stop ringing the bell."

I said, "What is the point of it all? Neither you nor the person who had come had any intention to be authentically sad or sorry. When I saw him, he was coming singing a song and smoking a cigarette. Anybody could see that he was in good spirits, enjoying the morning air, the fresh sun and the beautiful gardens all around"— because that place was in the most beautiful part of the city, and all the bungalows had gardens. "And just as he entered he threw away the cigarette, pulled his face down long, became sad. I was watching, and by chance this bell failed. And if he showed that he was so shocked, that was also hypocrisy, because he was not shocked. He was also pretending, just as you were pretending. The only man who was not pretending was me."

When the man went out he lit another cigarette—he did not think that I belonged to the family; I lived in the house, but he was not aware of the fact. And he started singing a film song and went away. I said to her, "Stop all this nonsense! Just simply say that you are relieved."

The woman had been suffering unnecessarily, there was no cure. Everybody was waiting for her death; the doctors were tired, they were also waiting for her death. They had said that there was no cure, but she could go on prolonging. She was very old. And it often happens that young people can die quickly, because death also needs a certain energy. Old people, very old people who should have died long before, don't even have the energy to die. They simply go on pulling. They have become so habituated to life, they have forgotten to die. In fact, what should have happened long before has not happened, they have missed their date. And perhaps, in the bureaucracy of death, everybody has forgotten about their file, too.

You know that as you go on longer in life, you will find that fewer people die. For example, at ninety, fewer people die than at seventy-five. At one hundred, even fewer people die. At one hundred and ten, rarely does somebody ever die. At one hundred and twenty, nobody dies—the file is forgotten, the man has forgotten to die. So here, everybody was relieved and still just kept showing a face which was not authentic.

This whole society has been created around a certain idea that is basically hypocritical. Here you have to be what others expect you to be, not what you are. That's why everything has become false, phony. Even in friendliness you are keeping a distance. Only so far do you allow anybody to come close.

People like Adolf Hitler . . . it is known that he never allowed anybody to put their hands on his shoulders. That much intimacy people like Adolf Hitler would not allow at all. They would like people to be far away; a distance that can allow them to pretend things. Perhaps, if somebody is very close, he may look behind your mask. Or he may recognize that it is not your face; it is the mask, your face is behind it.

So it is not only you, but everybody in the world in which we have been living who has been untrue and unauthentic.

My vision of a sannyasin is of a rebel, of one who is in search of his original self, of his original face. One who is ready to drop all masks, all pretensions, all hypocrisies, and show to the world what, in reality, he is. Whether he is loved or condemned, respected, honored or dishonored, crowned or crucified, does not matter; because to be yourself is the greatest blessing in existence. Even if you are crucified, you will be crucified fulfilled and immensely contented.

Just remember Jesus' last words on the cross. He prayed to

God, "Father, forgive these people who are crucifying me, because they know not what they are doing." He is not angry, he is not complaining. On the contrary, he is praying for them, that they should be forgiven. What a great dignity, what a man! A man of truth, a man of sincerity, a man who knows love and who knows compassion, and who understands that people are blind, unconscious, asleep, spiritually asleep. What they are doing is almost in their sleep.

Being an initiate into sannyas simply means the beginning of dropping all your masks. And that's what is gradually happening to you. You are feeling a new space . . . don't be impatient. You have been conditioned for so long, for so many years—your whole life—now unconditioning will also take a little time. You have been burdened with all kinds of false, pseudo ideas. It will take a little time to drop them, to recognize that they are false and they are pseudo.

In fact, once you recognize something as false, it is not difficult to drop it. The moment you recognize the false as false, it falls by itself. The very recognition is enough. Your connection is broken, your identity is lost. And once the false disappears, the real is there in all its newness, in all its beauty. Because sincerity is beauty, honesty is beauty, truthfulness is beauty. Just being yourself is being beautiful. And to me there is no other religion than this.

Just a little patience . . . what you have gathered in your sleep of many, many years, even if you wake up, the dust of dreams that you have gathered will take a little time to fall away. But your awareness, your understanding and your courage that you are determined and committed to find yourself, will dissolve all false faces that have been given to you by people. They are also unconscious—your parents, your teachers—don't be angry with them. They are also victims like you. Their fathers, their teachers, their priests, have corrupted their minds, and your parents and your teachers have corrupted you. All that you can do is: don't corrupt the younger children. Your children are your brothers and your sisters. Anybody whom you can influence, don't influence in a way that he becomes false; help the person to be himself.

What has been done in unconsciousness to you, you should not do to others—because you are becoming a little conscious, and each day the consciousness will grow. It needs nourishment, support; and being here with me and with all these fellow travelers, you can get immense support and nourishment. The whole atmosphere is to bring your authentic self out of all the clouds that have been covering you. But a little patience is certainly necessary.

You have never thought that what you are being taught by your parents—who love you—by your teachers, by your priests, could be wrong. But it has been wrong; it has created a whole wrong world. It has been wrong every inch, and the proof is spread all over history: all the wars, all the crimes, all the rapes . . . . Millions of people have been murdered, butchered, burned alive in the name of religion, in the name of God, in the name of freedom, in the name of democracy, in the name of communism—beautiful names. But what has happened behind those beautiful names is so ugly that one day man is going to look at history as if it were the history of insanity, not of a sane humanity.

Sannyas is an effort to at least make yourself sane and help others toward sanity. And the first step is, never pretend. Whatever the consequence, be true. However easy the hypocrisy may be, it is dangerous. It is dangerous because it is going to destroy your very spirituality, your very humanity. It is not worth it. It is better that everything should be taken away, but your dignity and your pride as a human being, as a spiritual being, should be left. That is more than enough to feel blissful and grateful toward existence.

—

The Genius Creates,
the Meditator Discovers

Osho,
When someone like Nietzsche or Gertrude Stein dies—
a genius who would probably have become enlightened if they
had met a master—what sort of consciousness do they carry
into the next life, and what was it that in their previous lives
allowed them to experience such a huge potential, such a great
flowering, and such a great knack? Was it the idea of wanting
to go their own way without a master?

There are many things in your question. First, you ask, "When
someone like Nietzsche or Gertrude Stein dies—a genius who would
probably have become enlightened if they had met a master—what
sort of consciousness do they carry into the next life?"

The first thing to be understood is that consciousness has
nothing to do with genius. Everybody can be a Gautam Buddha.
Everybody cannot be a Michelangelo, everybody cannot be a
Friedrich Nietzsche.

But everybody can be a Zarathustra, because the spiritual realization is everybody's birthright. It is not a talent like painting, or
music, or poetry, or dancing; it is not a genius either. A genius has
tremendous intelligence, but it is still of the mind.

Enlightenment is not of the mind, it is not intellect; it is intelligence of a totally different order. So, the first thing to remember is
that it is not only people like Friedrich Nietzsche who have missed
the journey toward their own selves; they were great intellectuals,
geniuses unparalleled—but all that belongs to the mind. And to be a
Gautam Buddha, a Lao Tzu, or a Zarathustra is to get out of the

mind, to be in a state of mindlessness. It does not matter whether you had a big mind or a small mind, a mediocre mind, or a genius; the point is that you should be out of the mind. The moment you are out of the mind, you are in yourself.

So the strange thing is that the more intellectual a person is, the farther he goes away from himself. His intellect takes him to faraway stars. He is a genius, he may create great poetry, he may create great sculpture. But as far as you are concerned, you are not to be created, you are already there.

The genius creates, the meditator discovers.

So, don't make a category of Nietzsche and Stein and Schweitzer separate from others. In the world of mind, they are far richer than you, but in the world of no-mind, they are as poor as you are. And that is the space which matters.

Secondly, you ask, "What sort of consciousness do they carry into the next life?" They don't have any consciousness to carry into another life. They have a certain genius, a certain talent, a certain intelligence; they will carry that intelligence into another life, but they don't have consciousness.

Consciousness is an altogether different matter. It has nothing to do with creativity, it has nothing to do with inventiveness, it has nothing to do with science or art; it has something to do with tremendous silence, peace, a centering—they don't have it. So the question of carrying a certain consciousness into the next life does not arise; they don't have it in the first place. What they have, they will carry into the next life. They will become greater geniuses, they will become better singers, they will become more talented in their field, but it has nothing to do with meditation or consciousness. They will remain as unconscious as you are, as anybody else is.

It is as if you all fall asleep here; you will be dreaming. Somebody may have a very beautiful dream, very nice, very juicy, and somebody may have a nightmare. But both are dreams. And when they wake up, they will know that the beautiful dream and the nightmare are not different—they are both dreams. They are nonexistential, mind projections.

When an ordinary man meditates, he comes to the same space of blissfulness as Nietzsche or Albert Einstein or Bertrand Russell. That space of blissfulness will not be different, will not be richer for Bertrand Russell because he is a great intellectual. Those values don't matter outside of the mind; outside of the mind, they are irrelevant.

This is great and good news because it means a woodcutter or a fisherman can become a Gautam Buddha. An uneducated Jesus, an uneducated Kabir, who doesn't show any indication of genius, can still become enlightened because enlightenment is not a talent, it is discovering your being. And the being of everyone is absolutely equal. That is the only place where communism exists—not in the Soviet Union, not in China.

The only place where communism exists is when somebody becomes a Gautam Buddha, a Zarathustra, a Lao Tzu. Suddenly all distinctions, talents of the mind, disappear. There is only pure sky where you cannot make any distinctions of higher and lower.

And you are asking, "What was it that in their previous lives allowed them to experience such a huge potential?"

You are growing every moment in whatever you are doing. A warrior will attain a certain quality of warriorness, a sharpness of the sword, and he will carry that quality into the next life. A mathematician will carry his mathematical intelligence to higher peaks in another life. That's why people are so different, so unequal, because in their past lives everybody has been doing different things, accumulating different experiences, molding the mind in a certain way. Nothing is lost, whatever you are doing will be with you like your shadow. It will follow you, and it will become bigger and bigger.

If Nietzsche is a great philosopher, he must have been philosophizing in his past lives—perhaps many, many lives—because such a genius needs a long, long philosophical past.

But the same is true about everybody. Everybody has a certain talent, developed or undeveloped; it depends on your decision, on your commitment. Once you are committed, you have accepted a responsibility to grow in a certain direction. Even whole races of people have developed in different directions, not only individuals.

For example, the Sikhs in India are not different from Hindus. They are only five hundred years old, following an enlightened man, Nanak. They became a different sect—but they are Hindus. And for these five hundred years, a strange phenomenon has happened, which has not happened anywhere else in the world. You cannot find in a Jewish family that one person is a Christian; you cannot find in a Mohammedan family that one person is a Hindu. But for five hundred years it has been a convention that in Punjab, where Sikhs dominate, the eldest son of a Hindu family should become a Sikh. He still remains in the family. His whole family is Hindu—his father is Hindu, his wife may be Hindu; he is a Sikh.

And the strangeness is that just by being Sikhs, the whole character of those Hindus has changed. Hindus have become cowards in the name of nonviolence; they are boiling with aggression within but, nonviolence is the ideal. Sikhs don't believe in nonviolence; neither do they believe in violence—they believe in spontaneity.

A certain situation may need violence and a certain situation may need nonviolence; you cannot make it a principle of life. You have to remain open, available, and responsive to the moment. And there is no difference of blood—the differences are such that one can only laugh at them—but they have created a totally new race.

Any Hindu can become a Sikh, any Mohammedan can become a Sikh, because the change is very simple. You have to have long hair, you cannot cut your beard or mustache; you have to use a turban, and you have to keep a comb in your turban; you have to wear a steel ring, a bracelet, just to show that you are a Sikh, and you have to carry a sword. You always have to wear underwear.

How these things have changed people is a miracle, because the Sikh is totally different from Hindus in his behavior. He is a warrior; he's not cowardly. He's more sincere, more simple, more of the heart.

It happened . . . I was going to Manali, the mountainous part, and it had rained, and the driver of my limousine was a Sikh. He started becoming afraid. The road was very small, the limousine was very big. The road was slippery; there were water pools collected on the road. At a certain point it looked very dangerous. A great river was flowing by, thousands of feet down—and just a small road. He stopped the car, went out, and sat there. And he said, "I cannot move anymore, it is simply going into death."

I said, "Don't be worried, you just sit; I will drive."

He said, "That is even more dangerous! I cannot give you the key."

I said, "This is very strange, because we have been traveling the whole night, twelve hours; now we are in the middle."

I tried to explain to him, "Even going back, you will have to travel twelve miles, twelve hours again on the same dangerous road. Whether you go backward or you go forward, it is the same."

He said, "It is not the same, because the road that we have passed, we have survived—I can manage. But ahead it seems to be simply committing suicide—I cannot go."

At that very moment, the inspector general of Punjab, who was coming to participate in the camp, came in his jeep. Seeing me standing there, and the limousine, and driver sitting there, he said, "What is the matter?"

I said, "It is good you have come at the right moment; this driver is not ready to move ahead."

The inspector general of Punjab was also a Sikh. He came close to the driver and told him, "You are a Sikh. Have you forgotten this? Just get into the car."

And strangely enough, he immediately got into the car. We moved. I asked him, "What happened? I have been arguing with you . . ."

He said, "It is not a question of argument. I am a Sikh! I am supposed not to be afraid, and I had forgotten it."

Just a slight idea can change not only the individual, it can change the whole race.

We have seen how Adolf Hitler created in Germany a race of warriors as nobody has done ever before, just by giving them the idea that "You are the purest Aryans," "You are born to rule all over the world." And once the idea got into their minds, he almost conquered the world. For five years, he went on conquering. People became so afraid that a few countries simply gave way to him without fighting. What was the point of fighting with those people? They were superhuman.

These ideas also are carried from one life to another.

In India there are sudras, untouchables. For five thousand years they have been condemned, oppressed, as nobody else in the whole world. I used to go to their functions and they would not let me sit with them. I would tell them, "You are as human as anybody else, and in fact you are doing a service which is far more valuable than any prime minister or any president of any country. The country would be more peaceful without these presidents and prime ministers, but without you, the country cannot live. You are keeping the country clean, you are doing the dirtiest jobs; you should be respected for it." They would listen to me, but I could see that they were not ready to accept the idea that they are equal to other human beings. For five thousand years they have not revolted against such oppression, such humiliation—

they just go on carrying it from one life into another life; it becomes more and more ingrained.

You are asking, "Was it the idea of wanting to go their own way without a master?" No, they had no idea of the great experience that happens between a master and a disciple. They have never consciously decided to go on their own way.

In fact in the West, masters have not existed. There have been saviors. They are not masters; they don't help you to become enlightened, they help you to remain unenlightened. Just believe in them and they will save you, you are not to do anything. The West has known prophets, messengers of God, but the West has not known masters. It has known mystics, but the mystics have remained silent in the West, seeing that they will not be understood. It is the atmosphere of thousands of years in the East that has made a few people take courage and say things which cannot be said. It was the long heritage that allowed a few mystics to become masters. The West has missed completely a whole dimension of life.

The East has also missed many things—it has missed the scientific mind, it has missed the technological progress. It has remained poor, it has been invaded very easily by anybody, because its whole soul was devoted toward only one thing—everything else was irrelevant: Who rules the country does not matter, what matters is whether you are enlightened or not. Whether you are rich or poor does not matter, what matters is whether you know yourself or not – a single-pointed devotion. And because of this, the East has a climate of its own.

As you enter the Eastern climate, you suddenly feel a difference. The West is more logical; the East is more loving. The West is more of the mind; the East is more of mindlessness, of meditation.

No, they have not missed a master; the very idea was nonexistent to them. Even today, millions of Western people are unaware of the fact of masters, disciples, meditation. It is only the younger generation—and that too a very small portion of it—which has entered the Eastern dimension, and has been shocked that the real richness is not of the outside world, the real richness is of the inside.

Ginsberg is dying. "Call the priest," he says to his wife, "and tell him I want to be converted into the Catholic religion."

"But Max, you are an orthodox Jew all your life. What are you talking about? You want to be converted?"

Ginsberg says, "Better one of them should die than one of us."

People have lived as Jews, as Christians, as Mohammedans, but people have not lived as simply religious. In the East also, only a very few people have lived in pure religiousness. But only those very few people have filled the whole of the East with a fragrance which seems to be eternal.

God asked Moses to choose whatever promised land he wished. After weighing several factors, Moses settled on California. But Moses, according to legend, had a speech impediment and he began to answer, "C . . . C . . ." Whereupon God said, "Canaan? That wasteland!? Well, okay Mo. If you want it, you got it."

Poor Moses, because of a speech impediment he got Canaan— which is now Israel; its old name is Canaan. But from the very beginning in the Western mind, the desire was for California. He could have asked for Kashmir, where finally he came and died; he could have asked for the land of Gautam Buddha. But the East has appealed only to those who are called by psychologists "introverts," and the West has appeal for those who are known as extroverts.

Going Eastward means going inward; going Westward means going outward. For thousands of years, authentic seekers have been coming to the East. They have found a certain magnetic pull. Where so many people have meditated, they have created a tremendous energy pool. Being in that atmosphere, things become simpler . . . because the whole atmosphere is supportive, is a nourishment.

I have been around the world and I have seen how the West is absolutely unaware of the Eastern grace. How is it that the Western man is unaware of himself? He's thinking of the farthest star, but not about himself. The East has remained committed to a single goal— to be oneself and to know oneself. Unless you know yourself, and you are yourself, your life has gone to waste; it has not blossomed, it has not flowered. You have not fulfilled your destiny.

The Bell Tolls for Thee

Osho,
In the last days [following the Chernobyl nuclear reactor
disaster in 1986—ed.] I often have the feeling that the ground
is going beneath my feet. It seems to me as if all that I love or
loved in the past is being destroyed. It is suddenly painfully
clear how fragile and mortal everything is. My parents, my son,
my brother and sister, my friends and my beloveds—all are in
danger. It is so hard for me to conceive that there is nothing
but the moment. I am fearfully asking myself, "What is going
to happen next?" But who is asking whom? All seems so
absurd and empty. Sometimes I even feel I am going mad.

Times of disaster make you aware of reality as it is. It is always
fragile; everybody is always in danger. Just in ordinary times you
are fast asleep, so you don't see it: you go on dreaming, imagining
beautiful things for the coming days, for the future. But in moments
when danger is imminent then suddenly you become aware that
there may be no future, no tomorrow—that this is the only moment
you have.

So times of disaster are very revealing. They don't bring anything new into the world; they simply make you aware of the world
as it is—they wake you up. If you don't understand this, you can go
mad; if you understand this, you can become awakened.

I am reminded of a story:

One great warrior, one of the best swordsmen of his country,
had a very obedient servant. He loved the servant, trusted him. He
was away, and the servant committed some mistake . . . which is

just human. When the warrior came back, he was so angry that he challenged the servant to have a fight with him, a duel with swords. He does not want just to kill him; the mistake that he has committed is big enough, although he may not understand that. He has spoiled one of the great paintings while cleaning it. The warrior said, "Because I have loved you, I will not kill you. I will give you a chance: you have to fight with me. Take this sword and come to the dueling ground."

The servant said, "You know, lord, that I don't even know how to hold a sword. It is better you kill me; you will kill me anyway— you are a famous swordsman. I cannot in any way be victorious in the fight."

But the master was stubborn. He said, "You will have to fight."

Then the servant said, "You will have to wait at least one hour. I will have to go to my master with whom I have been learning meditation—just to pay him respects, last respects, because I don't think I can survive fighting you." He was allowed the time. He went to the master.

The master laughed. He said, "Don't be worried. This is a good opportunity for you, because it is absolutely certain that he is a great warrior and he is going to kill you. You don't know anything about swordsmanship, so you will be killed.

"You don't have any future, you don't have any possibility of victory—you have only this moment. Why not be total at least once in your life? I know your man, the warrior: he will not leave you alone if he has said he will do it. But he has given you a chance, and I think it is a great opportunity."

The servant could not understand. He said, "What opportunity is there? He will simply kill me! I don't know even how to hold the sword, and he is one of the champions. It will be just a game to him."

The master said, "That is the point. He will think you are just a servant; what can you do? He will not be afraid of death; he will not be thinking that there is no tomorrow. He will still have tomorrow and the future. He will be in the ordinary sleepiness. You will not be.

"You don't have any tomorrow, you don't have any future: this is the moment, and you have nothing to lose. You are going to die, so why not be total and give him a good fight? And don't be worried about whether you know swordsmanship or not. Use this moment with total intensity."

Meanwhile, the whole neighborhood had gathered. The servant came. The warrior of course was totally on the ordinary level of sleepiness—it was just a joke for him to kill that man.

But it was not a joke for the servant; it was a question of life and death. He fought so furiously, so totally, that the master started retreating. He had never seen . . . he had been fighting his whole life, but he had never seen such a fighter! All those warriors whom he had faced were all living in the ordinary reality, as asleep as he was; there was no fear that the future is finished or tomorrow is not going to come.

But for the servant everything has come to an end, so why not do your best? He knew nothing of the art—but when the end is there, who cares whether you are doing right attacks or wrong attacks? And that made the warrior even more afraid. He knew how to fight with people who knew the art—but this man knew nothing. He was simply hitting him on this side, on that side, without understanding anything about what he was doing! He was total and intense, because this moment is the last moment and he does not want to hold on to anything. For what?—because the next moment is death.

So he was fully awake—his whole being was total and inte- grated—and he defeated the master. He did not kill him, but the master fell. And as the servant was putting his sword on the master's chest he asked, "Now what do you want? I have always loved you, I cannot kill you. But do you accept defeat or not?" And for the first time in his whole life, the warrior accepted defeat.

Thousands of people witnessed the scene. They could not believe that an ordinary servant has managed it. And not only that he was victorious—in that very moment he dropped the sword and told his master, "Now I am no longer your servant; I have found my way. I am grateful to you, I will always remain grateful to you; it was because of you that I became awake." He became an enlightened man. In that moment he tasted the fullness of being, the very peak of being.

It depends on you how you use the moment: you can panic, you can go mad, you can break down in fear, in tears. But that is not going to help your family or your friends or your beloved. It is not going to help you, either. This has simply created a situation in which those who have a little intelligence can start devoting more and more of their time to meditation, because tomorrow is really uncertain. It has always been uncertain, but now it is more uncertain than ever. This disaster may be just the beginning of a chain of disasters, because all these nuclear plants don't have any intrinsic safety. If anything goes wrong – and now we know that one plant has gone wrong—then they don't have any power, they are simply helpless. They cannot control the energy that they are creating.

The same disaster can happen in America, can happen in Germany. Just next to this plant which has burned down there are two other plants of the same age; they were made at the same time and had the same architect. They must have the same faults. There is every possibility that the second plant will blow up soon, and the third will not be far behind. And these disasters can trigger panic in thousands of people who are working in other plants; they can lose their so-called controlled behavior. They can start committing mistakes that they have never committed, just out of a feverish, frenzied state. And it is only a question of pushing a wrong button.

But you can use this as a great moment.

We are all, always, in danger.

You know the old saying: "Never send to ask for whom the bell tolls. It always tolls for thee." When somebody dies, the church bell informs the whole village. But never send anybody to ask for whom the bell tolls; it always tolls for thee, whoever may have died right now. Each death is your death, because each death is a reminder that you are not going to be here forever. Each death is an opportunity to be awake. Before death comes, use the opportunity of life to attain something which is beyond death.

It is pointless to be worried, because you will be simply missing this moment and you won't help anybody. And it is not that only your parents and your friends, your beloved, are in danger: the whole world is in danger. It is only a question of time. Somebody is in danger today, somebody else will be in danger tomorrow—but the danger is there. So learn the secret of how to transcend the danger. The secret is, start living more fully, more totally. Be more alert so that you can find within yourself something that is unreachable by death. That is the only shelter, the only security, the only safety. And if you want to help your friends and family, let them become aware of this secret.

What has happened is going to happen again and again, because there are so many nuclear plants, even in undeveloped countries which don't have the technical know-how, which are technologically still in the bullock-cart age, almost two or three thousand years back. They are not contemporaries, so these latest technical developments are very strange for them. But they have to develop them because others are developing, and the competition and the fear . . . And this has happened in Russia, where they are technologically contemporary. What will happen if it happens in Pakistan or in India? They don't have any technological sensibility. There is such a distance between them and nuclear technology that it cannot be bridged. American and Russian technologists can go and make a plant and hand it over to them, but for them it is going to be difficult.

There are going to be disasters. This is just the beginning. Use the opportunity to be awake—that's all you can do. There is nothing else that you can do.

And tell your friends to use the moment for meditation, because the disaster that has happened in the nuclear plant in Chernobyl near Kiev is not something that happens and is finished. Its effects will linger for decades, at least for thirty years. So it is not a question of some house being burned, and finished . . .

Around Kiev, particularly in the Ukraine where Kiev is, the Ukraine is the most productive part of the Soviet Union for wheat, for other foodstuffs. But now for thirty years you will not be able to grow anything in the Ukraine near Kiev. For thirty years the radiation will affect fruit, vegetables, wheat, and milk, because cows will be eating the grass. And any living things—grass, wheat, fruit—catch the radiation immediately; it becomes part of them. And when you eat, it becomes part of your system. There may be thousands of women who are pregnant. If the radiation has entered them, their children may be born distorted, blind, crippled, with no brain—anything is possible. The best will be that they are born dead; anything else is going to be a lifelong tragedy. So it is a danger not only for the living but even for those who are going to be born. And the same is true about animals. If they are pregnant their children will be crippled.

And governments go on lying. You can see how much politicians can lie. Another accident like that . . . and it all depends on the winds. You cannot control it; the winds can take the clouds, the fumes, the radiation in any direction, to any country, to anywhere. So it is not only a question of one place and its surroundings being affected. The place may be anywhere and you may be thousands of miles away but you can be affected because the winds can carry radiation. And you will be more vulnerable because you will not be so alert about it, and you will not take any precautions.

The danger is great, but as life is itself always in the grip of death, it is a good opportunity to be aware. Otherwise your death comes without any pre-information: suddenly it comes and you don't have even a single moment. And even in cases where death is certain—in cancer, or in AIDS—the doctors, the family, the friends, everybody tries to hide the fact that it is so close. With good intentions, but good intentions won't do—they are harming the person. The person should be made aware: "Your death is going to come within one month. You don't have any more life, so this month, do the best thing that can give you a taste of immortality."

Then, when you die there is no sadness, no misery—you simply move from this body into another body, or if you become enlightened . . . A sudden awareness of death can make you enlightened. So it is only a question of how to use everything—whatever it is. Use it rightly. The disaster is great, the danger is great, but great is the opportunity, too.

—

Every Crowd Is a Motley Crowd

Osho,
What is a beautiful and enlightened chap like you doing with a
motley crew such as we? (Actually, I don't really want to know
what you are doing, just please don't stop doing it!)

Every crowd is a motley crowd, but no individual is motley. Every
individual is an authentic consciousness. The moment he becomes
a part of the crowd, he loses his consciousness; then he is dominated by the collective, mechanical mind. You are asking me what I
am doing? I am doing a simple thing—bringing out individuals from
the motley crowds, giving them their individuality and dignity.

I don't want any crowds in the world. Whether they have gathered in the name of religion, or in the name of nationality, or in the
name of race, it does not matter. The crowd as such is ugly, and
the crowd has committed the greatest crimes in the world.

Because the crowd has no consciousness. It is a collective
unconsciousness.

Consciousness makes one an individual—a solitary pine tree
dancing in the wind, a solitary sunlit mountain peak in its utter glory
and beauty, a solitary lion and his tremendously beautiful roar that
goes on echoing for miles in the valleys.

The crowd is always of sheep; and all the efforts of the past have
been to convert every individual into a cog in the wheel, into a dead
part of a dead crowd. The more unconscious he is, and the more his
behavior is dominated by the collectivity, the less dangerous he is.

In fact, he becomes almost harmless. He cannot destroy even
his own slavery. On the contrary, he starts glorifying his own

slavery: his religion, his nation, his race, his color. These are his slaveries, but he starts glorifying them.

As an individual, he belongs to no crowd. Every child is born as an individual. But rarely does a man die as an individual.

My work is to help you meet your death with the same innocence, with the same integrity, with the same individuality as you have met your birth.

Between your birth and your death your dance should remain a conscious, solitary reaching to the stars—alone, uncompromising, a rebellious spirit. Unless you have a rebellious spirit, you don't have a spirit at all. There is no other kind of spirit available.

And you can rest assured that I am not going to stop! That's my only joy, to make as many people as possible free from their bondages, dark cells, their handcuffs, their chains. To bring them into light, so they can also know the beauties of this planet, the beauty of this sky, the beauties of this existence. Other than that, there is no God, and no God's temple.

In freedom you can enter the temple. In a collectivity, in a crowd, you simply go on clinging to the corpses of the past. A man living according to the crowd has stopped living. He is simply following like a robot.

And the man in the crowd has always behaved blindly. If you pull the same man out of the crowd and ask him, "What were you doing? Can you do it alone, on your own?" he will feel embarrassed. And you will be surprised to hear his answer: "On my own I cannot do such a stupid thing, but when I am in a crowd something strange happens."

For twenty years I lived in a city which was proportionately divided, half and half, into Hindus and Mohammedans. They were equally powerful, and almost every year riots happened. I used to know a professor in the university where I was teaching. I could never have dreamed that this man could put fire to a Hindu temple; he was such a gentleman—nice, well educated, well cultured. When there was a riot between the Hindus and the Mohammedans I was watching, standing by the roadside. Mohammedans were burning a Hindu temple, Hindus were burning a Mohammedan mosque.

I saw this professor engaged in burning the Hindu temple. I pulled him out and I asked, "Professor Farid, what are you doing?"

He became very embarrassed. He said, "I'm sorry, I got lost in the crowd. Because everybody else was doing it, I forgot my own responsibility—everybody else was responsible. I felt for the first time a tremendous freedom from responsibility. Nobody can blame me. It was a Mohammedan crowd, and I was just part of it."

On another occasion, a Mohammedan's watch shop was being looted. It was the most precious collection of watches. An old Hindu priest was there. The people who were taking away those watches and destroying the shop—they had killed the shop owner—were all Hindus. An old priest I was acquainted with was standing on the steps and shouting very angrily at the people, "What are you doing? This is against our religion, against our morality, against our culture. This is not right."

I was seeing the whole scene from a bookstore, on the second floor of a building just in front of the shop on the other side of the road. The greatest surprise was yet to come. When people had taken every valuable article from the shop, there was only an old grandfather clock left—very big, very antique. Seeing that people were leaving, the old man took that clock on his shoulders. It was difficult for him to carry because it was so heavy. I could not believe my eyes! He had been preventing people, and this was the last item in the shop. I had to come down from the bookstore and stop the priest. I said to him, "This is strange. The whole time you were shouting, 'This is against our morality! This is against our religion, don't do it!' And now you are taking the biggest clock in the shop."

He said, "I shouted enough, but nobody listened. And then finally the idea arose in me that I am simply shouting and wasting my time, and everybody else is getting something. So it is better to take this clock before somebody else gets it, because it was the only item left."

I asked, "But what happened to religion, morality, culture?"

He said this with an ashamed face—but he said it: "When nobody bothers about religion, culture and morality, why should I be the only victim? I am also part of the same crowd. I tried my best to convince them, but if nobody is going to follow the religious and the moral and the right way, then I am not going to be just a loser and look stupid standing there. Nobody even listened to me, nobody took any notice of me." He carried that clock away.

I have seen at least a dozen riots in that city, and I have asked individuals who have participated in arson, in murder, in rape, "Can you do it alone, on your own?" And they all said, without any exception, "On our own we could not do it. It was because so many people were doing it, and there was no responsibility left. We were not answerable, the crowd was answerable."

Man loses his small consciousness so easily in the collective ocean of unconsciousness. That is the cause of all wars, all riots, all crusades, all murders.

Individuals have committed very few crimes compared to the crowd. And the individuals who have committed crimes, their reasons are totally different—they are born with a criminal mind, they are born with a criminal chemistry, they need treatment. But the man who commits a crime because he is part of a crowd has nothing that needs to be treated—all that is needed is that he should be taken out of the crowd. He should be cleaned; he should be cleaned from all bondages, from any kind of collectivity. He should be made an individual again, just as he had come into the world.

The crowds must disappear from the world. Only individuals should be left. Then individuals can have meetings, individuals can have communions, individuals can have dialogues. Right now, being part of a crowd, they are not free—not even conscious enough to have a dialogue or a communion.

My work is to take individuals out from any crowd, Christian, Mohammedan, Hindu, Jew; any political crowd, any racial crowd, any national crowd, Indian, Chinese, Japanese. I am against the crowd and absolutely for the individual, because only the individual can save the world. Only the individual can be the rebel and the new man, the foundation for the future humanity.

The teacher is asking three boys in her class, "What was your mother doing when you left for school this morning?"

"Doing the washing," says Tom.

"Cleaning the bedroom," says Dick.

"Getting ready to go out and shoot ducks," says Harry.

"What! What are you talking about, Harry?" asked the teacher.

"Well miss," says Harry, "my dad has left home, and she threw her knickers on the fire and said she was going back to the game."

People are imitators. People are not acting on their own grounds; they are reacting. The husband has left her; that brings a reaction in her, a revenge—she is going back to the game. It is not an action out of consciousness, it is not an indication of individuality. This is how the collective mind functions—always according to somebody else. Either for or against, it does not matter; either conformist or nonconformist, it does not matter. But it is always directed, motivated, dictated by others. Left to himself, he will find himself utterly lost—what to do?

I am teaching my people to be meditators, to be people who can enjoy aloneness, to be people who can respect themselves without belonging to any crowd; who are not going to sell their souls for any awards and honors and respectability or prestige that the society can give to them. Their honor, their prestige, and their power is within their own being—in their freedom, in their silence, in their love, in their creative action—not in their reaction. What others do is not determinative of their life; their life springs from within themselves. It has its own roots in the earth and its own branches in the sky. It has its own longing to reach to the stars. Only such a man has beauty, grace. Only such a man has fulfilled the desire of existence to give him birth, to give him an opportunity. Those who remain part of the crowd have missed the train.

—

Terrorism Is in Your Unconsciousness

Osho,
Is the rise of terrorism over the last decade in some way
symbolic of what is happening to society in general?

Everything is deeply related with everything else that happens. The
event of terrorism is certainly related with what is happening in
the society. The society is falling apart. Its old order, discipline,
morality, religion, everything has been found to be wrongly based. It
has lost its power over people's conscience.

Terrorism simply symbolizes that to destroy human beings does
not matter, that there is nothing in human beings which is indestruc-
tible, that it is all matter—and you cannot kill matter, you can only
change its form. Once man is taken to be only a combination of
matter, and no place is given for a spiritual being inside him, then to
kill becomes just play.

Nations are irrelevant because of nuclear weapons. If the whole
world can be destroyed within minutes, the alternative can only be
that the whole world should be together; now it cannot remain
divided. Its division is dangerous, because division can become war
any moment. The division cannot be tolerated. Only one war is
enough to destroy everything, hence there is not much time left for
man to understand that we should create a world where the very
possibility of war does not exist.

Terrorism has many undercurrents. One is that because of the
creation of nuclear weapons, the nations are pouring their energies
into that field, thinking that the old weapons are out of date. They
are out of date, but individuals can start using them. And you cannot

use nuclear weapons against individuals—that would be simply stupid. If an individual terrorist throws a bomb it does not justify that a nuclear missile should be sent.

What I want to emphasize is that the nuclear weapon has given individual people a certain freedom to use old weapons, which was not possible in the old days because the governments were also using the same weapons.

Now the governments are concentrated on destroying the old weapons, throwing them into the ocean, selling them to countries which are poor and cannot afford nuclear weapons. And all those terrorists are coming from these poor countries—with the weapons that have been sold to their countries. And they have a strange protection: you cannot use nuclear weapons against them, you cannot throw atom bombs at them.

They can throw bombs at you and you are suddenly impotent. You have a vast amount of atomic bombs, nuclear bombs in your hands—but sometimes where a needle is useful, a sword may not be of any use. You may have the sword; that does not mean that you are necessarily in a superior position to the man who has a needle, because there are purposes in which only the needle will work—the sword will not be of any use.

Those small weapons from the old times were piling up, and the big powers had to dispose of them. They could drown them in the ocean, which meant so much money, so much manpower, so much energy would go to waste, that economically it was disastrous. But just to go on piling them up was also economically impossible. How many weapons can you gather? There is a limit. And when you get a new way of killing people more efficiently, then the old simply has to be got rid of.

It was thought that it would be better to sell them to poor countries. Poor countries cannot create nuclear weapons—it costs too much. And these weapons were coming cheap, as help. They accepted them, but those weapons cannot be used in a war. In a war those weapons are already useless. But nobody has seen the possibility that those weapons can be used individually, and a new phenomenon—terrorism—can come out of it.

Now a terrorist has a strange power, even over the greatest powers. He can throw bombs at the White House without any fear because what you have is too big and you cannot throw it at him. And his weapons are the weapons sold by you! But the phenomenon was not conceived of, because human psychology is not understood.

My understanding is that the way he has lived, man needs a war every ten to twelve years. He accumulates so much anger, so much rage, so much violence, that nothing short of a war will give him release. So, there is war after war, with a gap of only ten to fifteen years. That gap is a kind of relaxation. But again you start accumulating because the same psychology is working—the same jealousy, the same violence.

Man is basically a hunter; he is not by nature vegetarian. First he became a hunter, and for thousands of years he was just a meat-eater, and cannibalism was prevalent everywhere. To eat human beings caught from the opposing tribe you were fighting was perfectly ethical. All of that is carried in the unconscious of humanity.

Religions have imposed things very superficially on man; his unconscious is not in agreement. Every man is living in a disagreement with himself. So whenever he can find a chance for a beautiful cause—freedom, democracy, socialism—any beautiful word can become an umbrella to hide his ugly unconscious, which simply wants to destroy and enjoys destruction.

Now a world war has become almost impossible; otherwise there would have been no terrorism. Enough time has passed since the Second World War; the third world war should have happened nearabout 1960. It has not happened. This has been the routine for the whole of history, and man is programmed for it.

It has been observed by psychologists that in wartime people are happier than in peacetime. In wartime their life has a thrill; in peacetime they look bored. In wartime, early in the morning they are searching for the newspaper, listening to the radio. Things may be happening far away, but they are excited. Something in them feels an affinity.

A war that should have happened somewhere between 1955 and 1960 has not happened, and man is burdened with the desire to kill, with the desire to destroy. It is just that he wants good names for it.

Terrorism is going to become bigger and bigger, because the third world war is almost impossible. And the stupid politicians have no other alternative. Terrorism simply means that what was being done on a social scale now has to be done individually. It will grow.

It can only be prevented if we change the very base of human understanding—which is a Himalayan task; more so because these same people whom you want to change will fight you, they won't allow you to change them easily. In fact they love bloodshed; they don't have the courage to say so.

In one of the existentialist's novels, there is a beautiful incident which can almost be said to be true:

A man is presented before the court because he has killed a stranger who was sitting on the beach. He had never seen the stranger. He did not kill him for money. He does not yet know how that man looked because he killed him from the back, just with a big knife. They had never met—there was no question of enmity. They were not even familiar; they had not even seen each other's faces.

The magistrate could not figure it out, and he asked the murderer, "Why did you do it?"

He said, "When I stabbed that man with a knife and a fountain of blood came out of his back, it was one of the most beautiful moments I have ever known. I know that the price will be my death, but I am ready to pay for it; it was worth it. My whole life I have lived in boredom—no excitement, no adventure. Finally I had to decide to do something. And this act has made me world famous; my picture is in every newspaper. And I am perfectly happy that I did it."

There was no need for any evidence. The man was not denying it—on the contrary, he was glorifying it. But the court has its own routine way: witnesses still have to be produced; just his word cannot be accepted. He may be lying, he may not have killed the man. Nobody saw him—there was not a single eyewitness—so circumstantial evidence had to be presented by the police.

One of them was that possibly this man had killed according to his past life and his background. When he was young, his mother died. And when he heard that his mother had died, he said, "Shit! That woman will not leave alone me even while dying! It is Sunday, and I have booked tickets for the theater with my girlfriend. But I knew she would do something to destroy my whole day—and she has destroyed it."

His mother had died and he was saying that she had destroyed his Sunday! He was going to the theater with his girlfriend, and now he had to go to the funeral. And the people who heard his reaction were shocked. They said, "This is not right, what are you saying?"

He said, "What? What is right and what is wrong? Couldn't she die on any other day? There are seven days in the week—from Monday to Saturday, she could have died any day. But you don't know my mother—I know her. She is a bitch! She did it on purpose."

The second evidence was that he attended the funeral and in the evening he was found dancing with his girlfriend in a disco. And somebody asked, "What! What are you doing? Your mother has just died."

He said, "So what? Do you mean now I can never dance again? My mother is never going to be alive, she will remain dead; so what does it matter whether I dance after six hours, eight hours, eight months, eight years? What does it matter?—she is dead. And I have to dance and I have to live and I have to love, in spite of her death. If everybody stopped living with the death of their mother, with the death of their father, then there would be no dance in the world, no song in the world."

His logic is very right. He is saying, "Where do you draw the demarcation line? After how many hours can I dance?—twelve hours, fourteen hours, six weeks? Where will you draw the line? On what grounds? What is the criterion? So it doesn't matter. One thing is certain: whenever I dance I will be dancing after the death of my mother, so I decided to dance today. Why wait for tomorrow?"

Such circumstantial evidence was presented to the court—that this man is strange, he can do such an act. But if you look closely at this poor man, you will not feel angry at him; you will feel very compassionate. Now, it is not his fault that his mother has died; and anyway, he has to dance someday, so it makes no difference. You cannot blame this man for saying ugly things: "She deliberately died on Sunday to spoil my joy," because his whole experience of life must have been that she was again and again spoiling any possibility of joy. This was the last conclusion: "Even in death she will not leave me alone."

And you cannot condemn the man for killing a stranger—because he is not a thief; he did not take anything from him. He is not an enemy; he did not even see who the man was he was killing. He was simply bored with life and he wanted to do something that made him feel significant, important. He is happy that all the newspapers have his photo. If they had published his photo before, he would not have killed; but they waited—until he killed they would not publish his photo. He wanted to be a celebrity, just an ordinary human desire. And he was ready to pay with his life to become known to the whole world, recognized by everybody for at least one day.

Until we change the basic grounds of humanity, terrorism is going to become more and more a normal, everyday affair. It will happen in the airplanes, it will happen in the buses. It will start happening in the cars. It will start happening to strangers. Somebody will suddenly come and shoot you—not that you have done anything to him, but just the hunter is back.

The hunter was satisfied in war. Now war has stopped and perhaps there is no possibility for it. The hunter is back; now we cannot fight collectively. Each individual has to do something to release his own steam.

Things are interconnected. The first thing that has to be changed is that man should be made more rejoicing—something which all the religions have killed. The real criminals are not caught. These terrorists and other criminals are the victims.

It is all the religions who are the real criminals because they have destroyed all the possibilities of rejoicing. They have destroyed the possibility of enjoying the small things of life; they have condemned everything that nature provides you to make you happy, to make you feel excited, feel pleasant. They have taken everything away; and if they have not been able to take away a few things because they are so ingrained in your biology—like sex—they have at least been able to poison them.

Friedrich Nietzsche, according to me, is one of the greatest seers of the Western world; his eyes really go penetrating to the very root of a problem. But because others could not see it—their eyes were not so penetrating, nor was their intelligence so sharp—the man lived alone, abandoned, isolated, unloved, unrespected.

He says in one of his statements that man has been taught by religions to condemn sex, to renounce sex. Religion has not been able to manage it; and man has tried hard, but has failed because it is so deeply rooted in his biology; it constitutes his whole body. He is born out of sex—how can he get rid of it except by committing suicide? So man has tried, and religions have helped him to get rid of it; thousands of disciplines and strategies have been used. The total result is that sex is there, but poisoned. That word poisoned is a tremendous insight. Religions have not been able to take away sex, but they have certainly been successful in poisoning it.

The same is the situation about other things: religions are condemning your living in comfort. Now, a man who is living in comfort and luxury cannot become a terrorist. Religions have condemned riches, praised poverty; now, a man who is rich cannot be a terrorist. Only the "blessed ones" who are poor can be terrorists—because they have nothing to lose. And because others have things they don't have, they are boiling up against the whole of society. Religions have been trying to console them.

But then came communism—a materialist religion—which provoked people and said to them, "Your old religions are all opium to the people, and it is not because of your evil actions in this life or in past lives that you are suffering poverty. It is because of the evil exploitation of the bourgeois, the super-rich that you are suffering."

The last sentence in Karl Marx's *Communist Manifesto* is: "Proletariat of the whole world unite; you have nothing to lose and you have the whole world to gain." You are already poor, hungry, naked, so what can you lose? Your death will not make you more miserable than your life is making you, so why not take a chance and destroy those people who have taken everything away from you? Take those things back, distribute them. What the religions have somehow been consoling people with, communism suddenly made them aware of—although it was wrong and it was cunning and it was a lie. It kept people in a state of being half asleep.

Now that means this world is never going to be peaceful if we don't withdraw all the rotten ideas that have been implanted in man. The first are the religions. Their values should be removed so that man can smile again, can laugh again, can rejoice again, can be natural again.

Second, it has to be put clearly before the people that what communism is saying is psychologically wrong. You are falling from one trap into another. No two men are equal; hence the idea of equality is nonsense. And if you decide to be equal, then you have to accept a dictatorship of the proletariat. That means you have to lose your freedom. First the church took away your freedom, God took away your freedom. Now communism replaces your church, and it will take away your freedom. And without freedom you cannot rejoice; you live in fear, not in joy.

If we can clean the basement of the human mind's unconscious—and that's what my work is. It can be cleaned away: the
terrorism is not in the bombs in your hands; the terrorism is in your
unconscious. Otherwise, this state of affairs is going to grow more
bitter. It seems all kinds of blind people have bombs in their hands
and are throwing them at random.

The third world war would have released people for ten or fifteen
years. But the third world war cannot happen because if it happens
it won't relieve people, it will only destroy people.

So individual violence will increase—it is increasing. And all
your governments and all your religions will go on perpetuating the
old strategies without understanding the new situation.

The new situation is that every human being needs to go
through therapy, needs to understand his unconscious intentions,
needs to go through meditation so that he can calm down, become
cool, and look toward the world with a new perspective—of silence.

—

Freedom and Love, the Center and Circumference

Osho,
Thank you so much for your teachings. I am very grateful.
I came here very hungry and you are feeding me. My question
is: I have been raised to believe that commitment is absolutely
necessary if a relationship is to work. How can two people be
committed to each other? How does a relationship work? I am
afraid of commitment, so I avoid relationships. What is really
necessary in a loving relationship?

The first thing to understand is that I have no teachings. I am not
teaching you anything at all, because teaching simply means conditioning your mind—in other words, programming you in a certain
way. What I am doing here is just the opposite of teaching you: creating a space where you can unlearn whatever you have been
taught up to now. I am not a teacher.

That's the difference between a teacher and a master. The teacher
teaches, the master helps you to undo whatever the teachers have
done. The function of the master is just the opposite of the teacher.

The teacher serves the society, the establishment; he is the
agent of the past. He works for the older generation. He tries to condition the minds of the new generation so they can be subservient,
obedient to the past, to all that is old—to their parents, to the
society, to the state, to the church. The function of the teacher is
anti-revolutionary, it is reactionary.

The master is basically a rebel. He is not in the service of the
past, he is not an agent of all that you can think of as the establishment—religious, political, social, economic. His whole effort is to

help you to discover your individuality. It has nothing to do with tradition, convention. You have to go within, not backward. He is not in any way interested in forcing you into a certain pattern; he makes you free.

So what I am doing here is not a teaching.

That is a misunderstanding on your part, but it happens because you have lived with teachers, all kinds of teachers. It is rare to come across a master because society does not allow the master to happen.

The society is very afraid of the master; otherwise why did society poison Socrates? For what? He is the master par excellence, has never been surpassed by any other. His crime was that he was a master, and the society wanted him to be a teacher. He was helping people to discover the truth. And society is not interested in discovering the truth. It is interested in covering it more and more, because it lives through lies—it calls them beliefs.

All beliefs are lies; however beautifully presented, they are lies.

Truth cannot be given by one person to another. Only lies can be transferred, they are transferable.

Truth is nontransferable.

The master cannot hand over the truth to you, he can only create devices so that you can discover your own truth. It is always your own authenticity, your own being. Who can give it to you?

The teacher pretends to give you truth, but what he gives is just a decorated lie—although it may be very ancient, repeated for millions of years, so it appears like truth. Adolf Hitler, in his autobiography, *Mein Kampf*, says, "The only difference I know between a lie and a truth is that a truth is nothing but a lie often repeated." So you become hypnotized by it—and you can see it happening everywhere.

People are worshipping stones—people with eyes, people with intelligence, worshipping stones! They have been hypnotized from their very beginning. People believe in all kinds of stupidities, all kinds of superstitions, but they are not aware of it. They are almost in a drunken state, they are living in hypnosis. That is the secret of all hypnosis: repeat a thing again and again and again.

If you are consulting a hypnotist for any problem, his suggestion will always be to repeat something. If you are suffering from sleeplessness he will say, "Go on repeating, 'I am falling asleep, I am falling asleep, falling asleep. . .'" Go on repeating it and you will fall asleep. But that sleep will not be a natural sleep, it will be deliberately created. It will be false, it will be pseudo; it will not have the spontaneity of real sleep. It is a mind phenomenon, imposed. You have forced yourself to fall asleep.

Mothers know it very well. When a child wants to get up and they want him to go to sleep, they start singing a lullaby. A lullaby is nothing but hypnosis. A small song, maybe of one or two lines, repeated again and again, creates boredom, and boredom is one of the best tranquilizers yet discovered. Anybody will fall asleep, tired of it.

You can go on repeating a certain lie in the same way—Adolf Hitler proved it with his propaganda. He propagated utter lies, and one of the most intelligent races on the earth, the Germans, believed him. The most learned race, the race which has given birth to great philosophers, thinkers, professors, scholars of the caliber of Immanuel Kant, Hegel, Fichte, Feuerbach, Karl Marx, fell into a deep hypnosis—the whole race! And not only ordinary people but a great giant like Heidegger, one of the most important philosophers of this age, fell into the same trap. He started saying that Adolf Hitler was right.

And what was Adolf Hitler saying? He was saying that the world was going to the dogs because of the Jews. Now, there is no relationship at all, no logic in it. The Jews have nothing to do with the world going to the dogs. In fact, the Jews had no country at that time, they were nowhere in power. They were the least responsible for the world going to the dogs—because without power how can you destroy humanity? But still the Germans believed it. They started believing it simply because of repetition: it was repeated so often.

At first Adolf Hitler was laughed at—people thought, "He is crazy! This is sheer nonsense!" But he was stubborn: he went on hammering, he didn't listen to their laughter. He was idiotic, he may not have even understood their laughter. He was an imbecile! He continued hammering and finally he was victorious, he convinced people.

That's how the whole art of advertising exists, just through repetition. When neon lights were discovered and advertisements were put in neon lights—"Lux Toilet Soap" or something else—in the beginning it was a fixed light, you could read it once. Soon psychologists suggested "Let it be flickering." It comes on, goes off, comes on, goes off, so by the time a person passes it he will have to read it at least twenty, thirty times—because it goes off, then again it comes on, you have to read it again. So it is better to put it on and off because twenty repetitions, thirty repetitions each time a person passes by, will be more effective. Repeat it on the television, on the radio, in the magazines, in the newspapers; repeat it everywhere. Wherever a person goes, let him come across "Lux Toilet Soap" and soon he is hypnotized. He goes to the market, to the shop, and he starts asking for Lux toilet soap and he believes that he is choosing it. Somebody else has chosen it for him.

All teachings are creating a certain kind of hypnotic state in you. The function of the master is to de-hypnotize you, to de-condition you, to de-program you, so that you can again be innocent like a child, so that you can again function from the state of not-knowing.

A drunkard, staggering home, kept hitting the trees which lined the pavement—once, twice, then again. Finally he stopped where he was and said to himself, "It's better...hic...if I wait for the parade to finish!"

That's how Christians are, Hindus are, Mohammedans are: all drunk on certain philosophies which have been repeated continuously. They are seeing things which are not and they are not seeing things which are.

An Irishman was walking along a street pulling a brick along by a string, when Police Constable O'Murray, doing his morning round, saw him and decided to humor him. "Nice dog you've got there, sir!" he said.

"Now, bless the Virgin Mary!" replied the Irishman. "You can see that's not a dog there, Constable, that's a brick on a string!"

"Oh, sorry, sir!" exclaimed the policeman and walked away.

The Irishman then turned to the brick and whispered, "We really fooled him, Rover, didn't we?"

I am not teaching anything here, I am taking away many things from you. The work is negative: it is not giving anything to you but taking many things away from you, so that only your natural being is left behind. That cannot be taken away. Only that which has been given to you can be taken away; that which you have brought with your birth is intrinsic to you, it cannot be taken away. The master leaves you utterly naked, and in that nakedness is beauty, in that nakedness is truth, in that nakedness is freedom. In that nakedness is love and bliss, and all that for which the heart longs, and all that can make your life significant and meaningful.

You say, "I am very grateful. I came here very hungry and you are feeding me." That is far better than calling what I am doing a teaching. It is closer to the truth, it is more approximately true. It is a feast! I am sharing my being with you, not any teaching.

Your question is: "I have been raised to believe..." That's the whole problem of all human beings: everybody is raised to believe in something. No parents are yet capable of loving their children so much that they can leave them without conditioning them. They talk about love, but it is all false. They themselves may not be aware of it, it is true—they may not know what they are doing, they are unconscious. Their parents have done something to them, they are doing the same to their children. People go on giving things to people that have been given to them. Their intentions may be good, but they don't have enough awareness. They are not alert, so they go on giving you beliefs.

In a better world no parent will give you any beliefs. Certainly he will give you courage to inquire, courage to adventure. He will sharpen your intelligence, so that when you come across a lie you can see it and when you come across a truth you can immediately recognize it, but he will not give you any beliefs. No parent, if he loves the child, can give beliefs because beliefs are poisonous. They destroy your intelligence, they destroy your courage, and they create prejudices in you.

The whole of humanity is full of prejudices—that's why we are suffering so much. There is no need for so much suffering, for so much darkness. The only reason this suffering exists is very simple: it is because everybody is so stuffed with beliefs and everybody is looking through those beliefs, not directly.

And whenever you start looking through beliefs you cannot see the real. The eyes have to be utterly empty to see the real. The ears have to be totally empty to hear the real, to hear the truth. If you are already preoccupied, possessed by certain ideas, then those ideas function as barriers. If you are looking through a certain prejudice then you impose it, you project it, then everything enters you distorted.

In the beginning days of science, scientists thought that our minds, our senses, were for gathering information from the outside world. They are doors; the world enters through those doors—the senses, the mind; they are bridges. But now the latest research has proved just the opposite: your senses don't function as doors, your mind does not function as a bridge. Because it is so full of beliefs, it functions in just the opposite way: it prevents reality from reaching you.

You will be surprised to know that ninety-eight percent of reality is prevented from reaching you by your mind and senses. Only two percent of reality reaches you—only that which fits your beliefs reaches you. Unless a man is totally free of beliefs, he cannot know the immensity of truth, the ecstasy of existence.

You say, "I have been raised to believe that commitment is absolutely necessary if a relationship is to work." Now, so many things are taken for granted—you have not inquired into them. And they will look very true, they will look logical. Sometimes logic can be very absurd. Sometimes your so-called learned people are the most stupid people possible.

A learned man went into his library to read, but he couldn't find his glasses. He looked and looked, but he couldn't locate the missing glasses. So he used the logic of his ancient people, reasoning thus:

"Hypothesis: Maybe someone came in and stole my glasses while I was having lunch. No! Why not? Because if it was someone who needed glasses to read with he would own his own, and if he didn't need glasses to read with, why would he steal mine?

"Second hypothesis: Maybe a thief stole my glasses, not to use but to sell. But to whom can you sell a pair of reading glasses? If the thief offers them to someone who needs glasses that man surely owns a pair already, and if the thief offers them to someone who doesn't use glasses, why should such a man buy them? No!

"So where does this take us? Clearly the glasses must have been taken by someone who needs glasses and had glasses but cannot find them. Why can't he find them? Perhaps he was so absorbed in his studies that, absent-mindedly, he pushed his glasses up from his nose to his forehead, then forgetting he had done so, took mine!"

The answer began to dawn on the scholar.

"I will push this reasoning even further," he thought. "Perhaps I am that man who needs glasses, owns glasses, and moved his glasses up to his forehead and forgot that he had done so. If my reasoning is correct, that's where my spectacles ought to be right now."

And with that he moved his hand up to his forehead right on top of his glasses. So he smiled, pushed them down, and went on with his reading.

Such a long route to discover your glasses sitting just on your head! But that's how the learned fools go—round and round, about and about—and they go on handing all these hypotheses over to others.

This is just a hypothesis, it is not a truth. And you have not inquired into it, you have simply accepted it.

You say, "Commitment is absolutely necessary..." It is absolutely unnecessary! In fact, with a commitment there is no possibility of love. Just the opposite is the truth—exactly the polar opposite, diametrically opposite to what you have been raised to believe. Your hypothesis is absolutely wrong, but then you have to inquire from the very beginning.

Why do I say that commitment is absolutely unnecessary—not only that but a positive hindrance to love? What does commitment mean? It means a promise for the future. Love is in the present and commitment is for the future. Love is today and commitment is for tomorrows. Love is always now, here, and the commitment is always then and there; they cannot meet.

The commitment is a promise that "I will behave in the same way tomorrow as I am behaving today." But how can you promise about tomorrow? You may not even be alive, and even if you are alive you may have changed totally; even if you have not changed, the other person may have changed totally. Tomorrow is unpredictable.

A very ancient Chinese story:

A king became very angry with his prime minister for certain reasons, and the king was a little crazy—he sentenced him to death. It was the custom of that country that whenever a person was going to be crucified, the king himself used to come and see him, and if he wanted anything, his last wish had to be fulfilled. And certainly this man had served him his whole life—he had been his prime minister—so he came to see him the day he was going to be crucified. He was going to be crucified in the evening, so the king came in the morning. He came on his beautiful horse.

The prisoner could see the horse outside through the window. The king came in, and the prisoner started crying; tears started rolling down his cheeks.

The king was surprised. He said, "You, and crying? I would never have thought or imagined it, not even in my dreams! You are such a man of courage, you have fought so many battles. Are you afraid of death?"

And the prime minister said, "No, I am not crying or weeping because of my death, I am crying because of the horse!"

The king said, "What do you mean? Why should you cry because of the horse? What has the horse done?"

The prime minister said, "I have never said it to anybody, not even to my wife, that when I was young I lived with an alchemist. He was a miracle man, and from him I learned the art of teaching a horse to fly. But only a certain kind of horse can be taught. I have been looking for that special kind of horse my whole life—I could not find it—and today you have brought the horse. This is the horse for which I have been looking my whole life, and this is my last day! I am crying because my whole life's search, my long, long apprenticeship with the alchemist, my arduous journey to the Himalayas to learn the art—all has gone in vain. And why did you bring this horse today? You could have come on another horse. At least I could have died in peace. Now I will be dying in great turmoil."

The king became enchanted with the idea that the horse could fly. If it were possible then he would be the only king in the whole world whose horse could fly! He asked, "How long will it take to teach the horse?"

The man said, "Only one year."

The king said, "Okay, I trust you. I know you are a trustworthy man, you will not escape. I give you one year. If you can teach the horse to fly, not only will you be released from this sentence of death but you will also get half my kingdom. And if the horse cannot fly, of course, after one year you will be killed, so there is nothing for me to lose. Take the horse and go home."

The prime minister took the horse and went home. The wife was crying because this was the last day. They were getting ready to go and see him after the king had left him. The children were crying, all the relatives had gathered and his friends had gathered. They could not believe their eyes when the prime minister arrived there on the horse.

They said, "What has happened? What happened? Tell us how you managed it. Have you escaped from the prison? But we know that this horse belongs to the king. How did you get hold of this horse?"

And the prime minister laughed and he said, "Let me tell you the whole story." He told the whole story.

The wife started crying even more loudly. She said, "I know that this is absolutely false. You don't know any art, you have never been to the Himalayas, you have never been an apprentice to any alchemist. Now it will be even harder for us. Now I will have to suffer this whole year! This evening it would have been finished; after a few days I would have settled—time heals everything. But a year...and death will be constantly hanging over our heads like a naked sword! And if you are so clever, then why did you ask for only one year? You could have said it would take twelve years."

The prime minister said, "You don't know the king. Twelve years would have been too long. I know him perfectly well—I have asked the maximum that was possible; more than that and I would have died today. But don't be worried, in one year anything can happen. The king can die, I can die, the horse can die! Everything is possible. A year is long enough—much is possible. And I am free! Don't be worried."

And the end of the story is unbelievable—all three died!

Tomorrow is uncertain, absolutely uncertain. How can you promise? What commitment? One can only be committed for the moment, but that is not commitment. One can only say, "Now I love you, tomorrow we will see! Perhaps yes, perhaps no. Tomorrow will decide."

Just think of yesterday, when you had not met this particular man that you have fallen in love with. Yesterday you had not even dreamed about him, today you have met him. Yesterday there was no idea of the man, and today you are ready to commit yourself. But who knows about tomorrow? You may come across a better man— then what?

Commitment is stupid. Man can only live in the moment, and love is a flower of the moment. It is commitment that has made love false. A plastic flower will be there tomorrow, the day after tomorrow, year in, year out. You can trust that it will be there—it is a plastic flower. But the real rose opens its delicate petals early in the morning, dances in the wind, in the rain, in the sun, and by the evening the petals have withered away, and tomorrow you will not find even a trace of it.

Do you think the plastic flower is better than the real rose? If you think that way you don't know love, you know only marriage. Marriage is a plastic flower, love is a real rose. Perhaps it may survive, perhaps it may not.

Commitment is impossible—commitment is lying! And if you make any commitment for tomorrow, then there are only two possibilities: either you will have to break it or you will have to deceive, pretend. That's what millions of people around the world are doing. Their marriages finished the day their honeymoon finished, but they are still living, married, pretending, telling each other, convincing each other, "I still love you." In thousands of ways they are trying to prove that they are true to their commitment. But every action—their faces and their being—shows that they are sad. Where is that joy, that dance, that celebration that love brings in its wake? But love has been dead long. They are living only in the nostalgia, in the memory of it, hoping that there may be a certain resurrection of it someday.

The whole world is living with masks, pseudo faces: pretending to be somebody that you are not, doing something which you don't mean, saying something which you don't mean. It is a very crazy world. Be aware of this craziness. And this whole craziness has come into existence because of our insistence that commitment is absolutely necessary—not only necessary, but, you say, "absolutely necessary."

Man cannot live up to absolutes—don't ask the impossible from poor man! You will destroy everything that is valuable and delicate in him if you ask for absolutes. And that's what we have been doing—asking for absolutes.

In a little town in Russia there were many more girls than boys. Consequently, the local matchmaker was having an easy time making good matches for the young men of the village, although the girls were often ending up with the poor end of the bargain.

A rather unpleasant man in the village, whose face matched his disposition, wanted a bride who possessed beauty, charm and talent.

"I have just the girl for you," said the matchmaker. "Her father is rich and she is beautiful, well-educated, charming. There is only one problem."

"And what is that?" asked the young man suspiciously.

"She has an affliction. Once a year this beautiful girl goes crazy.

Not permanently, you understand. It's just for one day and she doesn't cause any trouble. Then afterward she's as charming as ever for another year."

The young suitor considered. "That's not so bad," he decided. "If she's as rich and beautiful as you say, let's go to see her."

"Oh, not now," cautioned the matchmaker. "You'll have to wait to ask her to marry you."

"Wait? For what?" pursued the greedy man.

"Wait for the day she goes crazy!" came back the answer.

Once in a while people go crazy, and that is the time when they get married; that is the time when they commit themselves for their whole lives—but only in craziness.

And love is, in the ordinary way, something crazy. It is biological, instinctive, it is unconscious, it is hormonal. It is more chemistry than spirituality. That's why we can very easily change the man into a woman and the woman into a man. Just a few glands have to be changed, and the man becomes a woman and the woman becomes a man. It is such an easy phenomenon now, and in the future it is going to happen even more often—and then commitment will become even more difficult. Your wife may decide one day to become a man—then? Your husband may go for an operation and become a woman—then what are you going to do?

And I don't think people will miss such opportunities, because if you can live as a man for a few months or years, and then as a woman, and then again as a man, then you are living life multi-dimensionally; you will have a little more variety—one gets tired of being a man or a woman. So it is perfectly good—just for a change it is good—and you can see the other side of the story, too. If all men once in a while become women, then no man will ever say that woman is a mystery, that it is impossible to understand a woman, and no woman will think that man is a mystery. You can be a man and you can know the mystery from the inside. And if you can change a few times, you may simply get fed up with the same game, because you will know there is nothing in being a man because you have been a man, and you will know that there is nothing in being a woman—you have been a woman. And that may bring a great transcendence in the whole human consciousness—people will start simply becoming buddhas easily.

A buddha is one who goes beyond being a man and beyond

being a woman; he transcends all sexuality. Very few people have been buddhas in the past, perhaps this is the reason—because you remain intrigued with the mystery of the woman, and the woman remains intrigued with the mystery of the man. And there is not much mystery, only chemistry.

So what you call love is an unconscious biological force— you are at the mercy of a biological force. It comes and it goes. Neither can you bring it nor can you force it to remain, because it has nothing to do with your consciousness. But commitment is conscious, and what you are committing yourself to is unconscious. There is no link between the two.

I cannot say that commitment is absolutely necessary if a relationship is to work. And who has ever heard of a relationship working? No relationship ever works—only in the beginning, but by the time it really starts getting hold of you it is too late. In the beginning it is sweet, beautiful, because both partners are really possessed by the chemistry and the biology, and they are seeing things which nobody else can see.

When you fall in love with a woman, everybody laughs. They think, "This man has gone crazy!" People start asking, "What do you see in this woman?" People start asking the woman, "What do you see in this guy?" But lovers go on seeing things—all kinds of hallucinations. In a very ordinary girl's face a lover can see the moon! And the woman can see in her lover all kinds of gods! She cannot believe that such a love has ever happened before or is going to happen again— it is for the first time and the last time. That's why in every language there exists the expression "falling in love." It is really falling—it is falling from your intelligence, falling from your humanity. It is really falling into a ditch! And if you become committed, then you cannot get out of the ditch either. Commitment means, "I am falling forever," so the ditch is going to become your grave.

Marriages have become people's graves—and I have seen no relationship that works. What works is love, but love is a delicate flower; you cannot depend on it. What works is momentary. But under the impact of love you can become committed. And then you will repent, but then you cannot escape from the commitment. You have been brought up with these beliefs: you have to stick to your promise, you have to be consistent, you have to fulfill whatever word you have given. Now your whole life is wasted.

What works as far as love is concerned is momentary; it certainly works for the moment, but no relationship works.

Relatedness works, but not relationship, and you have to understand the difference between the two. Love, the moment it becomes a relationship, becomes a bondage. And when you are in bondage it is impossible for you to be festive, to be joyous. You can fulfill the duty, but duty is an ugly, four-letter word. Duty means now you are caught and you have to do it.

Love is not something that you do, it is something that happens; duty is something that you have to do. It is a drag! You become a martyr. You start carrying your cross on your own shoulders, and you may think that you are becoming a Christ. Look at all the husbands carrying crosses. Look at the wives. Nobody seems to be happy. They are continuously quarreling, continuously fighting, continuously destroying each other, reducing each other to commodities, to means. The wife is using the husband, the husband is using the wife. It may be for different purposes—the wife uses the husband for economic purposes, and the husband uses the wife for sexual purposes—but both are using each other. And how can one be happy when one is being used?

So the moment the husband says, "What about it tonight?" the wife immediately says, "I am suffering from a headache," or she goes into a tantrum or starts a quarrel. So when the husband wants to make love to the wife, he has to bring ice cream and a bouquet and a sari, or something economic; then it is business, then it is simple give and take. This is not working—you cannot say that the relationship is working.

Yes, if love becomes conscious, then there is a tremendous joy—it works.

Love ordinarily is unconscious and animal. If you make it conscious—that means love plus meditation—then there is a totally different quality to it, a different beauty, a different flavor; then it works. But it works because of consciousness, not because of love. And consciousness changes love from relationship into a relatedness; it changes it more into a friendliness. It is no longer a bondage, it gives freedom.

The moment you become meditative, you stop reducing the other to a thing. Then you are no longer a husband and the wife is no longer a wife, you are just two friends. There is no legal bond.

You live together out of freedom, out of joy. You want to share, that's why you live together. And if that sharing stops, you simply say good-bye to each other with great respect, gratitude, because whatever the other has done one has to be grateful for; there is no sourness about it.

Consciousness works both ways: if you live together it is a friendship, and friendship gives you freedom. You can be friendly with many people; there is no possessiveness in it. When love becomes friendliness there is no possessiveness in it, there is no exclusiveness in it, there is no jealousy in it. And when there is no jealousy, no possessiveness, there is freedom.

Freedom works, friendliness works. And the moment love starts giving freedom to the other, then there comes a tremendous fulfillment out of it, because the greatest desire of the human being is freedom, not love. If one has to choose between love and freedom, then the conscious person will choose freedom and the unconscious one will choose love.

Why did Buddha escape from his palace? There was enough love, in fact more—too much—than a man can digest. His father had gathered all the beautiful women available in his kingdom; he was surrounded by beautiful women. He escaped—he could see the bondage. A great desire for freedom arose in him.

That's why in the East the ultimate state is called "moksha": moksha means "absolute freedom"—it is a higher phenomenon. Jesus calls God "love"—it is a little bit lower. Buddha calls it "nirvana," "absolute freedom," so absolute that you are even free from yourself. Your self was a bondage, was a limitation. You are free from everything, even from yourself. It is pure freedom.

Freedom is the ultimate desire of man. Man comes to flowering only in freedom. Meditation will bring freedom.

And I am not against love; it is just one step lower than freedom, and it is beautiful to have love as a fragrance around you. Let freedom be your center and love be your circumference. Let love be the circumference and freedom the center, and you will have a total being, a whole being.

But relationship never works. You are asking me: "How can two people be committed to each other?" They cannot be. Commitment is toward existence, not toward each other. Commitment can only be toward the whole, not to each other.

"How does a relationship work?" you ask. It does not work—and you can see it everywhere. It only pretends to. People go on saying that everything is okay, everything is good. What is the point of showing one's misery? What is the point of showing one's wounds? One goes on hiding them. It is humiliating to show one's wounds, so people pretend that everything is going well. They go on smiling, they go on repressing their tears.

Friedrich Nietzsche is reported to have said, "I go on smiling and laughing for the simple reason that if I don't smile I may start crying." Smiling is a way to cover up tears: you shift your energy from tears to a smile so that you can forget your tears. But everybody is full of tears.

I have looked into thousands of people's lives, their relationships. It is all misery, but they are covering it up, pretending everything is going okay. A relationship does not work, cannot work.

And you say, "I am afraid of commitment, so I avoid relationships." You are perfectly right in being afraid of commitment and you are perfectly right in avoiding relationships, but don't avoid relatedness. Don't make any exclusive relationship, be friendly. Let love rise to the level of friendliness, let it be just your quality. Be loving. Don't make it a relationship, just be loving.

These are the three stages. Relationship is the lowest, it is animal. Love as a quality of your being. Just as you breathe, let love be, that is human. And love at its ultimate expression is not even a quality, you become love itself. Then it is not even like breathing, it is your very being; then it is spiritual. But the third possibility can happen only through meditation. That refinement is possible only if your energies go through the whole alchemy of meditativeness.

Meditate. Become more aware of what you are doing, of what you are thinking, of what you are feeling. Become more and more aware, deeply aware, and a miracle starts happening. When you are more aware, all kinds of beliefs start disappearing, superstitions dissolve, disperse, darkness evaporates and your inner being becomes full of light.

Out of that light, love is a friendliness. It is not a question of commitment at all; one lives moment to moment, intensely, passionately, totally. That is commitment as far as I am concerned—commitment to the moment, because the moment is the only reality there is. The past exists no longer, the future is not yet—existence knows only the present. To be committed to the present moment is to be committed to existence, and there is no other commitment necessary.

—

The Journey from Hope to Hopelessness

Osho,
It feels so hopeless. I feel ashamed to have been a sannyasin for ten years and still be in this state. I hesitate to ask for your help, because even your words become mechanical in me after a few repetitions. Would you please comment?

It is not yet hopeless enough. Just make it a little more hopeless.

There comes a point in hopelessness where you stop hoping. Hopelessness is, still—deep down—nothing but hope. Let the hope fail, completely and totally, and a dramatic experience arises out of that space when you don't have any hope.

. . . Because hope is another name of desire, another name of expectation, another name of ambition. And before you can realize yourself, all desires, all expectations, all ambitions must have failed you, must have left you alone. Hoping nothing, desiring nothing, expecting nothing—where will you be? There is no way to go out.

Hope is a way of going out, desire is a way of going away, ambition is a way to avoid going in. On the path, to be utterly hopeless, so hopeless that you stop hoping . . . Suddenly you are in, without taking a single step.

Hope is a kind of opium; it keeps you intoxicated. To tolerate the miserable present, your eyes remain fixed on a faraway star: your hope.

Millions of people live without finding themselves—not because of any sin that Adam and Eve committed, or that they committed in some of their past lives. The sin is that people go on looking in the future, and the present goes on passing by. And the present is the only reality—the future is a dream and, however sweet, dreams never come true.

Self-realization is not a dream. It is a realization in the present moment of your own being.

So don't be worried: you are on the right path, becoming hopeless. Go on more and more, exhaust hopelessness. Come to the optimum hopelessness. Then hope disappears automatically.

And when there is no hope, you are. When there is no hope, the present is.

An old spinster died, and her two old friends went to a stonemason to have a gravestone made. "And what message would you like to have on the stone?" asked the mason.

"Well," said one of the old maids, "It's quite simple really. We would like: 'She Came a Virgin, She Lived a Virgin, and She Died a Virgin.'"

The mason replied, "You know, you ladies could save a lot of money by just saying: 'Returned Unopened.'"

Most of the people return unopened, and nobody is responsible except themselves.

You are saying, "It feels so hopeless . . ." Not yet; otherwise even this question would not have arisen. There is still hope. You say, "I feel ashamed to have been a sannyasin for ten years, and still be in this state." That is your ego feeling hurt; otherwise you would feel humble, not ashamed. What is there to be ashamed of?

Life is not a small thing. It is so vast, and we are so small. The ocean is so big, and we have to swim in it just with our own small hands. Only those people who never start swimming, and go on standing on the bank looking at others should feel ashamed. One who has started swimming...ten years is nothing much, even ten lives are short. One should be so patient. It is your impatience that is feeling ashamed; it is your ego that is feeling ashamed. You should feel humble—humble before the vastness of existence, humble before the mysteries of life...just humble, a nobody. And in that humbleness, the ocean becomes small and your hands become bigger.

You say, "I hesitate to ask for your help . . ." You go on saying things which you don't mean. If you really hesitate, then why are you asking? In fact, hesitation is your question. You should ask a little more so that you can open up, so that you can become more exposed. Don't go on hiding yourself. What is the hesitation in asking? And you go on rationalizing everything within yourself; you have rationalized your hesitation.

Everybody hesitates to ask, and the reason and the rationalization are two different things. The reason for feeling hesitation is that one does not want to show one's ignorance. And every question shows your ignorance. One hopes that some other stupid person is going to ask the question, just wait . . . Because human reality is one, and human problems are one, and the search for oneself is one. So, someday, somebody is going to ask the question that you cannot gather courage to ask yourself.

But I want you to remember that even in asking there is something valuable. In asking, you are exposing your ignorance; in asking, you are accepting that you don't know; in asking, you are dropping your so-called knowledgeability.

To ask a question is more important than the question itself. The question may be anything—*xyz*—but the very asking is significant. You don't remain closed, afraid that somebody may know that you know not. Exposing yourself—that you are ignorant—all fear disappears. You become more human, and you become more intimate with everyone who is a fellow traveler, because the same is his situation. That is the reason why one hesitates.

But rationalizations are a totally different thing. You rationalize that, "I hesitate to ask for your help because even your words become mechanical in me after a few repetitions." What is the need of repeating them? One repeats a thing because one wants to make it mechanical.

In your mind, there is a robot part; if you repeat a certain thing, the robot part takes it over. Then you don't have to think about it; the robot part goes on doing it. You are unburdened of thinking, you are unburdened of responsibility.

And the robot part is very efficient; it is mechanical. It has its use, and it has its misuse. When you are working in the ordinary world, the day-to-day world, if you have to remember every day where your house is, who your wife is . . . if you have to search every day in the crowd looking into every face—who is your wife?— it will become a little difficult. The robot part takes over. It knows the way home; you need not think on every turn whether to go right or to go left. You go on listening to the radio, and your hands will go on turning the steering wheel exactly to your own porch.

If one has to think about everything, life will become too clumsy. Once in a while, it happens with a few people, who don't have a very strong robot part—and these are the people who are very intelligent, such that their whole energy moves into intelligence and their robot part is left starving.

Thomas Alva Edison is one of the cases to be considered. He was leaving and going to an institute to deliver a lecture on some new scientific project he was working on. Saying good-bye, he waved to his wife and kissed the maid. His chauffeur could not believe his eyes! But Edison's robot part was very, very small; his whole life energy was devoted to scientific investigations, where a robot part is not needed.

One day he was sitting and working on some calculations, and his wife came with the breakfast. Seeing him so involved, she left the breakfast by his side, thinking that when he sees it, he will understand why she has not disturbed him. Meanwhile, one of his friends came. Seeing him so absorbed, he also felt not to disturb him. Having nothing else to do, he ate the breakfast and left the empty dishes by his side. When Edison looked up and saw his friend, he looked at the empty plate and said, "You came a little late, I have finished my breakfast. We could have shared it."

The friend said, "Don't be worried . . ."

You say that everything becomes mechanical in you after a few repetitions. But why repeat? The repetition is a method to make a thing mechanical. Always do something fresh, something new, if you do not want to get caught in repetitions. But in ordinary life, repetitions are perfectly good.

As you enter the world of higher consciousness, repetitions are dangerous. There you need always a fresh mind, an innocent mind, which knows nothing and responds to a situation not out of the mechanical, robot part of your mind, but from the very living source of your life. Here we are not concerned about the mundane world, our concern is to raise the consciousness.

Don't repeat, don't imitate. Remember one thing: you have to respond always in a fresh way. The situation may be old, but you are not to be old. You have to remain young and fresh.

Just try new responses. They will not be as efficient as mechanical responses, but efficiency is not a great value in spiritual life... freshness is.

A rabbi and a minister were sitting together on a plane. The stewardess came up to them and asked, "Would you care for a cocktail?"

"Sure," said the rabbi. "Please bring a Manhattan."

"Fine, sir," said the stewardess. "And you Reverend?"

"Young lady," he said, "before I touch strong drink, I would just as soon commit adultery."

"I've changed my mind!" said the rabbi." "As long as there is a choice, I will have what he's having."

People are imitative, and imitation is bound to be unintelligent. They want to do exactly the things that others are doing. That destroys their freshness.

Do things in your own style; live your life according to your own light. And even if the same situation arises, be alert to find a new response. It is only a question of a little alertness, and once you have started enjoying . . . And it is really a great joy to respond to old situations always in a new way, because that newness keeps you young, keeps you conscious, keeps you non-mechanical, keeps you alive.

Don't be repetitive.

But when I am saying "don't be repetitive" I don't mean in the ordinary life, in the marketplace. There, repetition is the rule. But in the inner world, the freshness of your response is the law.

—

Epilogue: A Very Valuable Time

Osho,
It has been said that in times of great stress—social,
economic, religious—that great good is possible. Is this
formulation true?

Yes, a time of crisis is a very valuable time. When everything is
established and there is no crisis, things are dead. When nothing
is changing and the grip of the old is perfect, it is almost impossible
to change yourself. When everything is in a chaos, nothing is static,
nothing is secure, nobody knows what is going to happen the next
moment—in such a chaotic moment—you are free, you can change.
You can attain the innermost core of your being.

It is just like in a prison: when everything is settled, it is almost
impossible for any prisoner to get out of it, to escape from the
prison. But just think: there has been an earthquake and everything
is disturbed and nobody knows where the guards are and nobody
knows where the jailer is, and all rules have dissolved, and everybody is running on his own—in that moment, if a prisoner is a little
alert, he can escape very easily. If he is foolish, only then will he
miss the opportunity.

When the society is in a turmoil and everything is in crisis, a
chaos pervades—this is the moment, if you want, you can escape
from the prison. It is so easy because nobody is guarding you,
nobody is after you. You are left alone. Things are in such a shape
that everybody is bothering about his own business—nobody is
looking at you. This is the moment. Don't miss that moment.

In great crisis periods, always, much enlightenment has happened.

When the society is established and it is almost impossible to rebel, to go beyond, not to follow the rules, enlightenment becomes very, very difficult—because it is freedom, it is anarchy; in fact, it is moving away from society and becoming individual.

The society doesn't like individuals: it likes robots who just look like individuals but are not individuals. The society doesn't like authentic being. It likes masks—pretenders, hypocrites, but not real persons, because a real person is always trouble.

A real person is always a free person. You cannot enforce things on him; you cannot make a prisoner out of him; you cannot enslave him. He would rather lose his life than to lose his freedom. Freedom is more valuable to him than life itself. Freedom is the highest value for him. That's why in India we have called the highest value moksha, nirvana; those words mean freedom—total freedom, absolute freedom.

Whenever society is in a turmoil, and everybody is tending his own business—has to—escape! In that moment, the doors of the prison are open. Many cracks are in the walls, the guards are not on duty . . . one can escape easily. The same situation was at the time of Buddha, twenty-five centuries before. It always comes in a circle; the circle completes in twenty-five centuries.

Just as a circle completes in one year—again summer comes back; one year's circle, and the summer is back—there is a great circle of twenty-five centuries. Every time after twenty-five centuries, the old foundations dissolve; the society has to lay new foundations. The whole edifice becomes worthless; it has to be demolished. Then, economic, social, political, religious—all systems—are disturbed.

The new is to be born; it is a birth pain.

There are two possibilities:

One is the possibility that you may start fixing the old falling structure: you may become a "social servant," and you may start making things more stable. Then you miss, because nothing can be done: the society is dying. Every society has a life span, and every culture has a life span. Just as a child is born, and we know the child will become a youth, will become old, and will die—seventy years, eighty years, at the most a hundred years—every society is born, is young, becomes old, has to die. Every civilization that is born has to die.

These critical moments are moments of the death of the past, the old; moments of the birth of the new. You should not bother; you should not start supporting the old structure—it is going to die.

If you are supporting, you may be crushed under it!

This is one possibility, that you start supporting the structure. That is not going to work. You will miss the opportunity.

Then there is another possibility: you may start a social revolution to bring the new. Then, too, again you will miss the opportunity—because the new is going to come, you need not bring it. The new is already coming! Don't bother about it; don't become a revolutionary. The new will come. If the old is gone, nobody can force it to remain; and if the new is there, and the time has reached, and the child is ripe in the womb, the child is going to be born. You need not try any caesarean operation. The child is going to be born; don't bother about it.

Revolution goes on happening by itself; it is a natural phenomenon. No revolutionaries are needed. You need not kill the person; he is going to die himself. If you start working for a social revolution—you become a "communist," a "socialist"—you will miss. These are the two alternatives in which you can miss.

Or, you can use this time of crisis and be transformed, use it for your individual growth. There is nothing like a critical moment in history: everything is tense and everything is intense, and everything has come to a moment, to a peak, from where the wheel will turn. Use this door, this opportunity, and be transformed. That's why my emphasis is for individual revolution.

—

Appendix

The Universal Declaration of Human Rights

Adopted and Proclaimed by General Assembly Resolution 217 A (III) of 10 December 1948

Preamble

Whereas recognition of the inherent dignity and of the equal and inalienable rights of all members of the human family is the foundation of freedom, justice and peace in the world,

Whereas disregard and contempt for human rights have resulted in barbarous acts which have outraged the conscience of mankind, and the advent of a world in which human beings shall enjoy freedom of speech and belief and freedom from fear and want has been proclaimed as the highest aspiration of the common people,

Whereas it is essential, if man is not to be compelled to have recourse, as a last resort, to rebellion against tyranny and oppression, that human rights should be protected by the rule of law,

Whereas it is essential to promote the development of friendly relations between nations,

Whereas the peoples of the United Nations have in the Charter reaffirmed their faith in fundamental human rights, in the dignity and worth of the human person and in the equal rights of men and women and have determined to promote social progress and better standards of life in larger freedom,

Whereas Member States have pledged themselves to achieve, in co-operation with the United Nations, the promotion of universal respect for and observance of human rights and fundamental freedoms,

Whereas a common understanding of these rights and freedoms

is of the greatest importance for the full realization of this pledge,

(*) Voting: 48 for, including United States; 0 against; 8 abstentions (Eastern bloc, Saudi Arabia, and South Africa)

Now, therefore,

The General Assembly Proclaims this Universal Declaration of Human Rights as a common standard of achievement for all peoples and all nations, to the end that every individual and every organ of society, keeping this Declaration constantly in mind, shall strive by teaching and education to promote respect for these rights and freedoms and by progressive measures, national and international, to secure their universal and effective recognition and observance, both among the peoples of Member States themselves and among the peoples of territories under their jurisdiction.

Article 1

All human beings are born free and equal in dignity and rights. They are endowed with reason and conscience and should act toward one another in a spirit of brotherhood.

Article 2

Everyone is entitled to all the rights and freedoms set forth in this Declaration, without distinction of any kind, such as race, color, sex, language, religion, political or other opinion, national or social origin, property, birth or other status.

Furthermore, no distinction shall be made on the basis of the political, jurisdictional or international status of the country or territory to which a person belongs, whether it be independent, trust, non-self-governing or under any other limitation of sovereignty.

Article 3

Everyone has the right to life, liberty and security of person.

Article 4

No one shall be held in slavery or servitude; slavery and the slave trade shall be prohibited in all their forms.

Article 5

No one shall be subjected to torture or to cruel, inhuman or degrading treatment or punishment.

Article 6
Everyone has the right to recognition everywhere as a person before
the law.

Article 7
All are equal before the law and are entitled without any discrimination to equal protection of the law. All are entitled to equal protection
against any discrimination in violation of this Declaration and against
any incitement to such discrimination.

Article 8
Everyone has the right to an effective remedy by the competent
national tribunals for acts violating the fundamental rights granted
him by the constitution or by law.

Article 9
No one shall be subjected to arbitrary arrest, detention or exile.

Article 10
Everyone is entitled in full equality to a fair and public hearing by an
independent and impartial tribunal, in the determination of his rights
and obligations and of any criminal charge against him.

Article 11
(1)   Everyone charged with a penal offence has the right to be
presumed innocent until proved guilty according to law in a public
trial at which he has had all the guarantees necessary for his
defense.
(2)   No one shall be held guilty of any penal offence on account of
any act or omission which did not constitute a penal offence, under
national or international law, at the time when it was committed. Nor
shall a heavier penalty be imposed than the one that was applicable
at the time the penal offence was committed.

Article 12
No one shall be subjected to arbitrary interference with his privacy,
family, home or correspondence, nor to attacks upon his honor and
reputation. Everyone has the right to the protection of the law against
such interference or attacks.

Article 13

(1)   Everyone has the right to freedom of movement and residence within the borders of each state.

(2)   Everyone has the right to leave any country, including his own, and to return to his country.

Article 14

(1)   Everyone has the right to seek and to enjoy in other countries asylum from persecution.

(2)   This right may not be invoked in the case of prosecutions genuinely arising from non-political crimes or from acts contrary to the purposes and principles of the United Nations.

Article 15

(1)   Everyone has the right to a nationality.

(2)   No one shall be arbitrarily deprived of his nationality nor denied the right to change his nationality.

Article 16

(1)   Men and women of full age, without any limitation due to race, nationality or religion, have the right to marry and to found a family. They are entitled to equal rights as to marriage, during marriage and at its dissolution.

(2)   Marriage shall be entered into only with the free and full consent of the intending spouses.

(3)   The family is the natural and fundamental group unit of society and is entitled to protection by society and the State.

Article 17

(1)   Everyone has the right to own property alone as well as in association with others.

(2)   No one shall be arbitrarily deprived of his property.

Article 18

Everyone has the right to freedom of thought, conscience and religion; this right includes freedom to change his religion or belief, and freedom, either alone or in community with others and in public or private, to manifest his religion or belief in teaching, practice, worship and observance.

Article 19
Everyone has the right to freedom of opinion and expression; this right includes freedom to hold opinions without interference and to seek, receive and impart information and ideas through any media and regardless of frontiers.

Article 20
(1)   Everyone has the right to freedom of peaceful assembly and association.
(2) No one may be compelled to belong to an association.

Article 21
(1)   Everyone has the right to take part in the government of his country, directly or through freely chosen representatives.
(2)   Everyone has the right of equal access to public service in his country.
(3)   The will of the people shall be the basis of the authority of government; this will shall be expressed in periodic and genuine elections which shall be by universal and equal suffrage and shall be held by secret vote or by equivalent free voting procedures.

Article 22
Everyone, as a member of society, has the right to social security and is entitled to realization, through national effort and international co-operation and in accordance with the organization and resources of each State, of the economic, social and cultural rights indispensable for his dignity and the free development of his personality.

Article 23
(1)   Everyone has the right to work, to free choice of employment, to just and favorable conditions of work and to protection against unemployment.
(2)   Everyone, without any discrimination, has the right to equal pay for equal work.
(3)   Everyone who works has the right to just and favorable remuneration ensuring for himself and his family an existence worthy of human dignity, and supplemented, if necessary, by other means of social protection.

(4)   Everyone has the right to form and to join trade unions for the protection of his interests.

Article 24
Everyone has the right to rest and leisure, including reasonable limitation of working hours and periodic holidays with pay.

Article 25
(1)   Everyone has the right to a standard of living adequate for the health and well-being of himself and of his family, including food, clothing, housing and medical care and necessary social services, and the right to security in the event of unemployment, sickness, disability, widowhood, old age or other lack of livelihood in circumstances beyond his control.
(2) Motherhood and childhood are entitled to special care and assistance. All children, whether born in or out of wedlock, shall enjoy the same social protection.

Article 26
(1)   Everyone has the right to education. Education shall be free, at least in the elementary and fundamental stages. Elementary education shall be compulsory. Technical and professional education shall be made generally available and higher education shall be equally accessible to all on the basis of merit.
(2)   Education shall be directed to the full development of the human personality and to the strengthening of respect for human rights and fundamental freedoms. It shall promote understanding, tolerance and friendship among all nations, racial or religious groups, and shall further the activities of the United Nations for the maintenance of peace.
(3)   Parents have a prior right to choose the kind of education that shall be given to their children.

Article 27
(1)   Everyone has the right freely to participate in the cultural life of the community, to enjoy the arts and to share in scientific advancement and its benefits.
(2)   Everyone has the right to the protection of the moral and material interests resulting from any scientific, literary or artistic

production of which he is the author.

Article 28
Everyone is entitled to a social and international order in which the rights and freedoms set forth in this Declaration can be fully realized.

Article 29
(1)   Everyone has duties to the community in which alone the free and full development of his personality is possible.

(2)   In the exercise of his rights and freedoms, everyone shall be subject only to such limitations as are determined by law solely for the purpose of securing due recognition and respect for the rights and freedoms of others and of meeting the just requirements of morality, public order and the general welfare in a democratic society.

(3)   These rights and freedoms may in no case be exercised contrary to the purposes and principles of the United Nations.

Article 30
Nothing in this Declaration may be interpreted as implying for any State, group or person any right to engage in any activity or to perform any act aimed at the destruction of any of the rights and freedoms set forth herein.

United Nations Charter: Preamble

WE THE PEOPLES OF THE UNITED NATIONS DETERMINED
- to save succeeding generations from the scourge of war, which twice in our lifetime has brought untold sorrow to mankind, and

- to reaffirm faith in fundamental human rights, in the dignity and worth of the human person, in the equal rights of men and women and of nations large and small, and

- to establish conditions under which justice and respect for the obligations arising from treaties and other sources of international law can be maintained, and

- to promote social progress and better standards of life in larger freedom,

AND FOR THESE ENDS
- to practice tolerance and live together in peace with one another as good neighbors, and

- to unite our strength to maintain international peace and security, and

- to ensure, by the acceptance of principles and the institution of methods, that armed force shall not be used, save in the common interest, and

- to employ international machinery for the promotion of the economic and social advancement of all peoples,

HAVE RESOLVED TO COMBINE OUR EFFORTS TO ACCOMPLISH THESE AIMS

- Accordingly, our respective Governments, through representatives assembled in the city of San Francisco, who have exhibited their full powers found to be in good and due form, have agreed to the present Charter of the United Nations and do hereby establish an international organization to be known as the United Nations.

About Osho

Osho's unique contribution to the understanding of who we are defies categorization. Mystic and scientist, a rebellious spirit whose sole interest is to alert humanity to the urgent need to discover a new way of living. To continue as before is to invite threats to our very survival on this unique and beautiful planet.

His essential point is that only by changing ourselves, one individual at a time, can the outcome of all our "selves" – our societies, our cultures, our beliefs, our world – also change. The doorway to that change is meditation.

Osho the scientist has experimented and scrutinized all the approaches of the past and examined their effects on the modern human being and responded to their shortcomings by creating a new starting point for the hyperactive 21st Century mind: OSHO Active Meditations.

Once the agitation of a modern lifetime has started to settle, "activity" can melt into "passivity," a key starting point of real meditation. To support this next step, Osho has transformed the ancient "art of listening" into a subtle contemporary methodology: the OSHO

Talks. Here words become music, the listener discovers who is listening, and the awareness moves from what is being heard to the individual doing the listening. Magically, as silence arises, what needs to be heard is understood directly, free from the distraction of a mind that can only interrupt and interfere with this delicate process.

These thousands of talks cover everything from the individual quest for meaning to the most urgent social and political issues facing society today. Osho's books are not written but are transcribed from audio and video recordings of these extemporaneous talks to international audiences. As he puts it, "So remember: whatever I am saying is not just for you...I am talking also for the future generations."

Osho has been described by *The Sunday Times* in London as one of the "1000 Makers of the 20th Century" and by American author Tom Robbins as "the most dangerous man since Jesus Christ." *Sunday Mid-Day* (India) has selected Osho as one of ten people – along with Gandhi, Nehru and Buddha – who have changed the destiny of India.

About his own work Osho has said that he is helping to create the conditions for the birth of a new kind of human being. He often characterizes this new human being as "Zorba the Buddha" – capable both of enjoying the earthy pleasures of a Zorba the Greek and the silent serenity of a Gautama the Buddha.

Running like a thread through all aspects of Osho's talks and meditations is a vision that encompasses both the timeless wisdom of all ages past and the highest potential of today's (and tomorrow's) science and technology.

Osho is known for his revolutionary contribution to the science of inner transformation, with an approach to meditation that acknowledges the accelerated pace of contemporary life. His unique OSHO Active Meditations˜ are designed to first release the accumulated stresses of body and mind, so that it is then easier to take an experience of stillness and thought-free relaxation into daily life.

Two autobiographical works by the author are available:
Autobiography of a Spiritually Incorrect Mystic,
St Martins Press, New York (book and eBook)
Glimpses of a Golden Childhood,
OSHO Media International, Pune, India (book and eBook)

OSHO International Meditation Resort

Each year the Meditation Resort welcomes thousands of people from more than 100 countries. The unique campus provides an opportunity for a direct personal experience of a new way of living – with more awareness, relaxation, celebration and creativity. A great variety of around-the-clock and around-the-year program options are available. Doing nothing and just relaxing is one of them!

All of the programs are based on Osho's vision of "Zorba the Buddha" – a qualitatively new kind of human being who is able *both* to participate creatively in everyday life *and* to relax into silence and meditation.

Location
Located 100 miles southeast of Mumbai in the thriving modern city of Pune, India, the OSHO International Meditation Resort is a holiday destination with a difference. The Meditation Resort is spread over 28 acres of spectacular gardens in a beautiful tree-lined residential area.

OSHO Meditations
A full daily schedule of meditations for every type of person includes both traditional and revolutionary methods, and particularly the OSHO Active Meditations". The daily meditation program takes place in what must be the world's largest meditation hall, the OSHO Auditorium.

OSHO Multiversity
Individual sessions, courses and workshops cover everything from creative arts to holistic health, personal transformation, relationship and life transition, transforming meditation into a lifestyle for life and work, esoteric sciences, and the "Zen" approach to sports and recreation. The secret of the OSHO

Multiversity's success lies in the fact that all its programs are combined with meditation, supporting the understanding that as human beings we are far more than the sum of our parts.

OSHO Basho Spa
The luxurious Basho Spa provides for leisurely open-air swimming surrounded by trees and tropical green. The uniquely styled, spacious Jacuzzi, the saunas, gym, tennis courts...all these are enhanced by their stunningly beautiful setting.

Cuisine
A variety of different eating areas serve delicious Western, Asian and Indian vegetarian food – most of it organically grown especially for the Meditation Resort. Breads and cakes are baked in the resort's own bakery.

Night life
There are many evening events to choose from – dancing being at the top of the list! Other activities include full-moon meditations beneath the stars, variety shows, music performances and meditations for daily life.

Facilities
You can buy all of your basic necessities and toiletries in the Galleria. The Multimedia Gallery sells a large range of OSHO media products. There is also a bank, a travel agency and a Cyber Café on-campus. For those who enjoy shopping, Pune provides all the options, ranging from traditional and ethnic Indian products to all of the global brand-name stores.

Accommodation
You can choose to stay in the elegant rooms of the OSHO Guesthouse, or for longer stays on campus you can select one of the OSHO Living-In programs. Additionally there is a plentiful variety of nearby hotels and serviced apartments.

www.osho.com/meditationresort
www.osho.com/guesthouse
www.osho.com/livingin

For More Information

www.**OSHO**.com

a comprehensive multi-language website including a magazine, OSHO Books, OSHO Talks in audio and video formats, the OSHO Library text archive in English and Hindi and extensive information about OSHO Meditations. You will also find the program schedule of the OSHO Multiversity and information about the OSHO International Meditation Resort.

http://OSHO.com/AllAboutOSHO
http://OSHO.com/Resort
http://OSHO.com/Shop
http://www.youtube.com/OSHO
http://www.Twitter.com/OSHO
http://www.facebook.com/pages/OSHO.International

To contact OSHO International Foundation:
www.osho.com/oshointernational,
oshointernational@oshointernational.com